endorsements

In *People, Please!* Heather Seeger becomes the guide we've always needed to lead us out of the wilderness of people pleasing and into the full life of knowing that Jesus is (and always has been) pleased with us. Offering her own experiences with warm vulnerability, she's written a book that will help us walk in the freedom of doing good for the glory of God alone. And like the Israelites, God promises to be with us every step of the way!

Janet Ables, speaker, Bible teacher and author of
Faith Refined **and** *To Know Him by Name*

You're invited to sit down, take a breath — and then take off the mask. In *People, Please!*, Heather Seeger approaches her readers the way she approaches life—with honesty and candor, welcoming conversation and reflection as she shares the tender trap of the drive to be and do good. In each chapter, Heather considers how we might let go of our own need for goodness to lay hold of the goodness of God. She weaves stories from both the Old and New Testaments to help us see patterns and perspectives. And she invites us in to the vulnerability of a life being fully lived, with every question and doubt and glorious triumph.

Ronne Rock, storyteller and mentor, author of
One Woman Can Change the World

Heather Seeger has unearthed her own fears and found gold. *People, Please!* is a story of encouragement and leadership. In it, she shares her conviction, confidence and personal journey to help you lead a more full and confident life.

James Victore, creative and author of
Feck Perfuction: Dangerous Ideas on Business

endorsements

As a recovering 'people-pleaser' I was happy to read a book that pointed me back to the truth - that Jesus loves me and sets us free! Thank you Heather for sharing your story as you encounter the freedom given as a gift from Jesus! What a reminder to be brave and live differently!

Genevieve Epp

This book helped challenge me to see my own insecurities and trials in a new light. Turning them into praises for the Lord even in the times wondering in my "own desert".

Tabitha Hull

People, Please! invites us to join the Israelites as they travel through the wilderness. Along the way, Heather draws parallels between the Israelites and the modern-day struggle to trust God. Throughout this journey, we are called to release our pride, trust in God, and live freely in his daily grace.

Ellie Kirkland

I am thankful for the journey I got to go on with the Israelites. I was able to learn more about their 40-year journey while also acknowledging my own struggles with people-pleasing. This amazing book brought up things I needed to but hadn't addressed and it encouraged me to take those struggles to the Lord. I hope you enjoy learning through this book as much as I did!!

Ana McEuen

endorsements

I have watched Heather live out this book. She has helped me through my own "wilderness" and I can attest that she is a capable and wise guide. I wish this book existed 20 years ago, so we both could have been set free sooner! But I am grateful she has given all of us her words now. The world needs the people God created us to be, not the "be good", try-hard, pretending everything is "fine" us. This book will help us all step into our authentic selves and be released to do the work God created us for. Our families, communities, and world will be better because of it.

Lindsey Thomson

They say leaders must go first before they can expect others to do what they ask. I think the same can be said of writers. Words fall flat and lose their meaning if the writer hasn't been there and done that themselves. Heather puts herself out there in an authentic and beautiful way. In doing so, she invites the reader to bravely do the same and experience the wonder, awe, and all-encompassing love of Jesus.

Lindsey Zarob

People,
Please!

people, please!

Leaving the Crowd's Approval
for the Glory of One

Heather Seeger

PUNCHLINE
PUBLISHERS

Scripture taken from the NEW AMERICAN STANDARD BIBLE®, Copyright
© 1960, 1962, 1963, 1971, 1972, 1973, 1975, 1977, 1995 by The Lockman
Foundation. Used by permission.

First paperback edition July 2024

Cover design by Heather Seeger
Illustrations copyright © 2024 by Heather Seeger

ISBN 978-1-955051-36-1 (hardcover)
ISBN 978-1-955051-37-8 (paperback)
ISBN 978-1-955-51-38-5 (eBook)

Published in association with Punchline Publishers
www.punchlineagency.com

www.heatherseeger.com
@heather_seeger

To Eric, Ella, & Mia
Thank you for your encouragement, trust,
and love during these wild writing times.
Y'all are dope!

table of contents

author's note

I was surviving life, but my mind and soul felt off. Something was wrong. I felt I had to be on all the time. I felt used. I felt unfulfilled. I felt overwhelmed by people. I felt unworthy of people's time unless I was serving or doing something for them. I allowed others' words to shape me. I thought I had a lot to give, but I did not know how to show up and be myself without creating a new mask for each space I filled.

I had a problem with people-pleasing. I was being good by saying yes to almost anything to help fulfill others' expectations of me. I was not walking in the freedom God had given me.

I knew there was a possibility of learning to say no, to regain control and decide where God wanted me to say yes. I was tired of feeling like I was disappointing everyone. Where was my confidence? I was still looking to others for my identity. Could I know and believe my value by learning how Jesus saw me?

I needed to take a realistic look at myself. How could I stop idealizing and romanticizing my time? Why had my self-image become a source of shame? What was the probability of me learning to pay attention to God and not humans? How could I learn to hold things loosely?

Most mornings I asked God to show me what good he had for me that day. I journaled daily, reflecting on the past day. I read the Bible to help direct me and learn how Jesus walked the Earth. I learned to be still and listen to the Holy Spirit's prompting throughout the day. I opened my eyes to pay attention to those around me.

I attempted to rid myself of my people-pleasing by only saying yes to things I deemed "good for God's kingdom." I was doing good by saying "yes" to all those things, yet I was still exhausted. I had to learn to recognize the good work God put before me and accept that this good work could change over time. I grasped that, no matter what I did or did not do, God was pleased with me, just as I was.

Throughout this book, I will share my journey and how it parallels the Israelite's exodus from Egypt, walking through the wilderness, and entering the promised land. I invite you to journey slowly as you read so God can reveal what is causing your heart to ache or what is hindering you. My journey was slow, too, as he has revealed specific motivations and characteristics I needed to give him. I took time to reflect on my story, studied the

Israelites in the exodus, and examined Jesus' walk on Earth. God revealed the specific motivations and characteristics I needed to let go of and lay at his feet. I pray you will listen to the nudges of what God has for you.

God has refined me, but his work is not done yet. Knowing I need to change habits and thoughts is hard to admit. I feel regret for how I acted in some trials, but I have learned to accept my humanity. I have learned to wait, sit in the suffering, and dance for joy through the work God is doing in my life. I will have to forgive and ask for forgiveness. I will face the same trials most days, but how I approach them, with Jesus by my side, is a choice I get to make.

I do these hard things by remembering what God has done. The journey into this wilderness of change happens by reflecting on where God has shown up. The journey does not end when you put this book down. I want to show you how to do good for the glory of God and how to spur others around you to do the same. You can live your most alive life, but just a fair warning, it is not easy. We can make an impact in both great or mundane ways. May we leave the enslavement of people-pleasing and make our way into the wilderness to strip bad habits, build new ones, and learn to trust God as a provider and guide to living in freedom.

Part One

Be Good. How We Relate to Others

one

is this my best life?

I was a kid living my best outdoor life in Colorado. I could see the foothills of the Rocky Mountains from our home and get an even better view from my favorite spot at a park nearby. I grew up on bedtime stories of missionaries from the past and books on tape by Frank Peretti during road trips. These experiences sparked my imagination for spiritual things and a longing to travel the world. I remember wanting Jesus in my life, during a Christmas Eve service. Our pastor called all the children to the front and shared the good news of Jesus. After some time, I was baptized in the cold water of Chatfield Lake at a church picnic. The sky was cloudy and the water was choppy. I wore a giant white T-shirt; we probably had fried chicken and coleslaw from King Soopers.

We moved to Texas around the time I turned 10. Texas was the worst—not the people or where we lived—but the heat and everything outside the house wanting to eat us. My younger sister and I were homeschooling when we moved allowing us time to go on adventures and long road trips. In high school, we transitioned to public school. We had tried out a private school but didn't like it. I wanted to learn French and play in band while my mom was not excited about the math or the dissecting of things. I am sure there are other reasons to this decision, but I was happy with it! I had friends from church, so it wasn't hard to make that move, rather more of a fast track to learning about all the things in teenage culture. I grew up in the era of WWJD bracelets and True Love Waits. I learned of great moral behavior, how to always check off the "daily Bible reading" box, and the art of masking how you really feel. And, of course, how to be a good Christian girl by putting others first and myself last, always.

Life continued. As I grew in my relationship with Christ, I served in the church and lived life a little afraid of being my full self by changing or masking who I was to be just enough and not too much. When I applied for college, I felt the first groan of discontentment and that something was not right. Yet I ignored it and hid behind layers of people-pleasing masked as a Christian being good.

Years passed, I layered new masks as I took on more roles, and on I went into adulthood.

I had the hustle to get things done. I had Jesus. I saw all the people around me who needed help. So, I helped. I showed up for everyone. I said yes to everything. But I felt like a stranger in my skin. I had a hard time being quiet and still. In my "quiet time" with Jesus, I was just gleaning the surface for those go-to verses as quick prayers to get me through my busy day. I could not be vulnerable with friends and had difficulty expressing my emotions.

Perhaps I should introduce myself. Hi! My name is Heather, and I am a recovering people-pleaser. I am here to share my journey. My life didn't feel like the life of free-indeed that I knew Jesus promised us. It felt like I was living for everyone else. As a people-pleasing, be-gooder I asked, *Is this my best life?*

Before we get started, let's take some time to define "be good," as I will be using this synonymously with people-pleaser and people-pleasing.

While nothing is inherently wrong with that phrase, it can be loaded with meaning, presumptions, and perceptions. When I started writing this book, I used it because it felt like a less negative form of people-pleasing—a way of saving face. Also, I believe the way one translates "be good" will differ according to the one receiving or giving the instructions. For example, when I hear "be good," my automatic translation is...

"Be perfect. Let nothing bug you. Brush it off. No conflict allowed. Be agreeable. Be helpful beyond your capacity, and help everyone around you succeed. After all, you are here to serve and help. You don't need to be successful at what *you* want to do—look at what they are doing because of your help! Don't doubt. Don't worry. Don't tell anyone how you are doing. They don't need to know or want to hear your banter. Help *them* be happy. You'll feel happy because you helped them. Fall in line, swim with the stream. Don't go against the flow. Don't piss anyone off."

The above is the actual running commentary that happens in a flash in my head when "be good" is said or implied. Yes, I bring baggage to the phrase, but I know I am not alone. Saying "be good" may not be a big deal, or it could send someone into a negative spiral. We may not have to be politically correct with all our words and phrases, but we can be kind and do better by being aware of the person we are talking to before we speak.

When living a life to "be good" as defined above, you must keep up appearances. Wearing a mask is acceptable. You work to please everyone around you and generally forget about yourself. It is hard. It is stressful. And autonomy doesn't exist. You withhold pieces of yourself because you are afraid to show your full self. You feel that people may not like or approve of that person—the person you really are.

I've created a little checklist to help us think through what is to come in the following chapters. These are some ways I have behaved, withheld, or covered. I do not find them inherently wrong, but when I find my motivations behind the good works themselves become an idol. Jesus is no longer the center. It is me striving to "be good" for others. Yes, we will talk quite a bit about Jesus, and how he shows us what it looks like to live free of people-pleasing and striving to be good.

Here are a few characteristics that may ring true for you. Feel free to check them off physically or mentally or jot them down in a journal.

[ ] I am a fixer and will ensure you will not fail; let's come up with all the options.

[ ] I am a servant who will give up my comforts for your needs.

[ ] I am a helper! If you need it, I've got it, and I'm already in the car to come help.

[ ] I am a protector of those in my close circle of friends and family. Please don't mess with them.

[ ] I am not important enough to put myself first when needed.

[ ] I am joyful in appearance but not happy. I don't get to be happy. Fake it 'til you make it.

[ ] I am always distracting myself. I don't want to be alone with my thoughts.

[ ] YES TO ALL THE THINGS!

If you can check one, all, or some, then from my very (un) professional analysis, friend, you might be a people-pleaser, a "be gooder," if you will.

DISCLAIMER: Maybe this doesn't hit you at all. You're like, *This is not for me, but (someone's name here) could use this.* Well, feel free to share! Maybe you continue to read so you can remain mindful of how they receive and respond to your words and actions. Thanks in advance for sticking around to help a friend out.

We clarified what it means to "be good", now let's get our Bible understanding aligned. The Bible is books of the Old Testament (OT) and New Testament (NT) in one document. The Old Testament has 39 books which covers roughly 2,000 years of human history and people's interactions with God before Jesus was born. It is where we find the story of the Israelites navigating the wilderness. The New Testament has 27 books and picks up 400 years after the last book of the OT. The NT is about the life of Jesus and those who followed him during his life on Earth and what happened to this group of followers after he ascended to heaven after his resurrection—about 100 years of human history.

The Bible is full of grace. However, it is expressed differently by God in the OT and NT. Grace is God's favor to people in the OT. For example, Isaiah 30:18a says, "Therefore the Lord longs to be gracious to you, and therefore he waits on high to have compassion on you." In the NT, Grace is how we are saved through faith in Jesus. Ephesians 2:8-9 says, "For by grace you have been saved through faith; and that not of yourselves, it is the gift of God; not as a result of works, so that no one may boast." Grace is an ongoing gift renewed each day. We no longer have to find favor in God like in the OT because we live after Jesus, and he offers us the gift of salvation and grace.

Growing up, I loved going to Sunday school, especially when we had a particular teacher. He loved the history of the Bible. I enjoyed learning from him, and it sparked my interest in learning more about everything. I wanted to dive into the Word on my own and requested my first study Bible in middle school. I was captivated reading the verses and then researching what might be going on in the background.

The Old Testament is my favorite, and I have loved reading the crazy story of the Israelites. In high school and college, I was like, *These dummies can't see what's right in front of them!* As I have continued to study the Bible over the last few decades, I have learned I am far more like the Israelites than I want to admit.

At the beginning of this journey, I thought my similarities with the Israelites were a bummer. I would rather compare myself with Moses, their great leader. I began to loosen my grip on perfection and see myself as a lost little sheep, like the Israelites, wanting to stay in the comfort of the known instead of trusting God in the unknown.

I also began to learn to look at grace from a different perspective. I knew of grace, but thought it was a one-time deal, not something renewing each day. I especially did not think it was for someone like me—someone who lived trying to be good. I was living an Old Testament life in a New Testament world. I was pleasing people and temporarily feeling fulfilled by those actions. I thought I was being a good Christ-follower because I was serving everyone who asked for help.

Throughout this book, I'll share my story of what I learned from the Israelites' exodus from Egypt, just as I have shared a bit of where I am coming from—my context and history. A mini history lesson on the Israelites will also be helpful. The Israelites came to Egypt as a small family led by Jacob (Bible scholars use Israel after his name was changed by God in Genesis 22). They came because of a famine in their homeland. Egypt had food because of the second-in-command, Joseph—Jacob's long-lost-thought-to-be-dead-favorite-son (Genesis 37-50). The Pharaoh of that time allowed the whole family to move in and settle in the best land (Genesis 47:6). Their livestock was productive, and they multiplied. Hundreds of years passed, new pharaohs came and went, and their freedom was slowly pulled from them until they became enslaved builders. The rules and work got more intense, and their freedom was stripped. Yet, their number still grew.

After about 400 years, Pharaoh instituted new laws for population control and decided murdering baby boys was the way to do it. Pharaoh commanded the Jewish midwives to do the dirty work, but they believed and trusted God and helped the boys live. Moses was born during this unrest, and his mom knew he was special. She devised a plan with his sister, Miriam, to set him in the Nile, in the hope that Pharaoh's daughter would find him and adopt him. She did, so Moses grew up in the royal court but longed to be a part of his people and help them. He murdered an Egyptian to defend an Israelite and fled to Midian (Exodus 1-3).

This is where we will step into the story with the Israelites—tired, broken, and oppressed. Is this their best life? Absolutely not. Is there more to life than slavery and living under this rule and reign of terror? Yes, there is! God heard them crying out to him and knew it was time to act, so he called Moses back to Egypt to lead them (Exodus 2:24-25, Exodus 3:7-9).

They did not know what would happen if they followed Moses, nor did they want to follow him at first. They did know they were mistreated, but they had food and somewhere to sleep. They were not keen on the idea of leaving, but in the end, when Pharaoh said leave, they went (Exodus 4-12). As they left, they had no idea that God planned to take them the long way around to the promised land. God knew that if they came to the land of the Philistines and went straight into battle, they would die, or worse, they would run back to Egypt and forgo their promised land (Exodus 13:17-18, 20-22).

If you have taken the time to read or listen to these verses in the Bible, you may have questions, such as, why not go the fastest way? Hadn't they been through enough as slaves for hundreds of years? Of course! Yet, if we look at the map, they would have been heading straight into war. They may have moved their bodies out of Egypt, but God knew they were not spiritually ready for a battle. They needed some time with God in the wilderness to bond with their Creator. To understand who God was and what he had for them. They needed to build their capacity for future battles—both physically and spiritually.

We are told in Exodus 13:20-22 that God guided them by a cloud by day and fire by night. They had physical guidance, God's presence, every day showing them which way to go. Just because they could see his glory, it did not make their journey any easier. Remember, they were going into the *wilderness*. It was not meant to be a habitable, kind place for a whole nation to live in, but it would be a place where they would rely on God in ways they never had before.

God had in mind that they would take time to be restored to their full selves before fighting and living in the promised land. Much like going to therapy, they would cut through the layers and begin healing. I think of Shrek as he talks about his emotions in the form of layers of an onion. This kind of work—peeling and prepping can be stinky and make you cry.

We will learn all about their trials as we walk through this book and how much we must also rely on God. I hope you can pay attention to the parts of your story that may parallel the Israelites actions and attitudes toward God. I hope you will know God is paying attention to you. I hope that sharing my story will be a helpful example of how to see the same hope in your own life.

In short, God was giving them a better end. He wanted to see them succeed, so he built in time for growth. He knew casting them into a giant battle would only lead to discouragement, so much so, that they would want to return to slavery. (We know this because they say it several times in the 40 years of being in the wilderness.)

Much like how the Israelites might have felt in their oppression during their slavery in Egypt, I felt like God wasn't showing up as my time in college was ending. I met Eric during the first week of classes my sophomore year of college. I had just transfered from a community college. I thought he was cute, but at the time I was mad at boys. We ended up being in some of the same classes, then ministry, and friends. As I wrapped up college, Eric and I were getting married. He would be finishing school and I graduated the same weekend we got married. And I needed a job. I became anxious and worried. I felt like everyone would judge me if I choose poorly. I had been praying and journaling and reading my Bible, but there was no clarity. With uncertainty, I made a choice. I ended up loving the work, but not who and what it was for. I was looking for something more which led me to feel miserable, insecure, and doubt all the things I thought I knew about being a grown-up with Jesus. I had learned that, if I was close to God, he would help me in my decisions. I did not fully understand how God gave us choices. I needed some lessons in grace and confidence in my faith.

I continued to move through life like this: obsessing over what people thought of me, being loyal, and having a hard time saying "no" because I might not be the go-to person anymore. Above all, hoping and praying I was making the decision that God wanted me to make on the "perfect" path he had set before me. I would look around me, see what people were saying and doing, and apply it to my life. It was incredibly demanding on my heart and soul.

I was bogged down with memories of shame for not living up to people's expectations or my expectations of myself. I was trying to figure out how to communicate with God and understand what the hell was going on in this adulting Christian life.

In early 2013, I came across *Grace for the Good Girl* by Emily P. Freeman. I loved it! I hated it! And, yes, I even threw it at the wall! But it was God's way of gently saying, "I hear you and see you." It was his act of grace toward me, and it helped me begin my journey into the wilderness. I was able to shift my perspective—mostly about myself and my relationship with God. Freeman lit my world on fire and allowed me to see how much I was living my life to please people. She writes about living in grace. Not just grace as a one-time thing when we accept Jesus—grace as an ongoing thing. It felt like the concept of grace as a constant, everyday thing was something I missed through the many years of sermons, Sunday school lessons, and Bible studies.

Grace.
Living without fear of what others think of you.
Grace.
What God gives us, and we do not deserve.
Grace.

It helped remind me that this "be good" girl was made new. Every day. I began a journey of believing God had given me grace each morning and learning how to live like I believed that truth.

The clarity I was seeking from God was: *How do I live my life if I must also do everything for everyone else?* God helped me name the problem with this question. Knowing the question helped guide my first steps on this path into the wilderness. The Israelites were not put on the fastest route to their promised land, and neither was I!

As we will see later in this journey, at times, the Israelites wanted to return to their old lives in Egypt because it was all they knew. They did not know they were made for more. They were fine with their "be good" life of working for a pharaoh who cared nothing for them. They were comfortable even though they were uncomfortable.

The Israelites saw God's goodness, believed, and turned their hearts towards him. When things got uncomfortable, they started to believe they knew their needs better than God. They would cycle through this thinking again and again. Cycles of being in awe, trusting, then turning. The same cycles I found myself in. It's a *wicked cycle* (think Boston accent, not evil, but also not great). We'll explore it as we move through the chapters.

So now that you know I love the Bible and the Israelites, I'm going to show you how I wandered the wilderness. In my journey (and I think yours too), I'll explore leaving the enslavement of people-pleasing, taking off the mask of being good, and making my way into the wilderness to strip the bad habits and build new ones, and to trust God as provider and giver of a life free-indeed.

I am excited for you and your journey as you read this book. While the book may be a quick read, the journey and lessons will hopefully last much longer. I hope you will find quiet space and room in your life to mark your journey. I hope and pray you see that God has paid attention to your story and wants to guide and walk with you in this journey.

Don't be afraid of the hardships that you may encounter along the way. This journey will have bumps, fits of anger, and tears. Maybe you'll throw this book at the wall! It will also have shouts of praise, jumps of joy, and times of celebration and laughter with your community as you look back and see all God has revealed and done. Glory.

I promise it is worth it.

YOU ARE WORTH IT. Most importantly, GOD SAYS YOU ARE WORTH IT!

things to think about

I hope and pray God shows up for you
and you can notice how he is moving.

1. What does "be good" or people-pleasing bring
   to mind when you hear the phrase?

2. Do you think your current life is your best life?
   Why or why not?

3. Who are you living for? Yourself, others, God?

two

trusting God in the unmasking

I was doing what I thought God had called me to do. Saying
"yes" to the things that sounded important, where I thought
people needed the most help from me—in work, volunteering, and friendship. With all this doing, I had a running
soundtrack in my head still telling me how unimportant I was
in all those things. Deep down this was an issue of trust and
pride (low self-esteem). I thought I was unimportant because
I could not trust God. I knew he would guide me, show me how
to fix things in my life, and ask me to serve people.

When I did all these things, I felt alone. No matter what
I did, I always felt like I was still watching my back and thinking
things like, *Did I mess up? Was that enough?* Or making sure that
I followed directions to a T and wondered, *Will I get blessed
from this?* These thoughts showcased my legalistic background

and the unfortunate idea that if you believe in God, give to him and do what he says, you will be rewarded (usually financially). It kept me guessing if I was good enough at being good, or if I was going to have an upset God who was not proud of the work I was doing.

Okay, here we go. My first big question: Does God ask us to be good? As a reminder, here is *my* definition of being good (or people-pleasing):

> When living a life to "be good," you keep up appearances. You work to please everyone around you and generally forget about yourself. It is hard. It is stressful. And autonomy doesn't exist. You withhold pieces of yourself because you are afraid to show your full self. You feel that people may not like or approve of that person.

In fact, I have found the opposite to be true. Being "good" can imply near perfection by human standards, but God asks us to follow his direction, to walk in obedience. If we look to Jesus' life as our example, he wasn't being good, he was doing good and being disruptive. He lived the first 30 years of his life quietly. There is not too much recorded of his upbringing in the New Testament. But when he began the work he came to do, he did not live quietly. The people he called to follow him were some of the least educated or liked in the Jewish community. He spoke of grace, love, and justice for all. He spoke to the most religious leaders with authority, pointing to the works they did that held no meaning because of their pride. He did not follow the rules of religion. He turned them on their head, showing people the new, free way they could live if they followed him. Does the Bible tell us to be good? Why are we telling people (and ourselves) to be good? Because of expectations? To receive praise? Should we tell people to be good? Or are those the wrong questions?

Is the right question: Does God ask for obedience? Is this the obedience defined by our culture, or something different and holy?

Does being good and everything it entails leave no room for you? What does it keep you from doing or being? Do we trust what God says about who we are?

From the research I have done, I have concluded that God does not ask, demand, or imply that we be good or be people-pleasers. There are many commands with "be" at the beginning, but they go like this: be of good cheer, be strong and courageous, be at peace, etc.

Ecclesiastes 5:18 is the closest "be good" statement. "Here is what I have seen to be good and fitting: to eat, to drink and enjoy oneself in all one's labor in which he toils under the sun during the few years of his life which God has given him; for this is his reward." King Solomon, one of the wisest people in the Bible (despite his faults), wrote this after exploring all the things this world had to offer. Some may find his whole book a bit cynical, but I find it refreshing. When we drop the cares of pleasing others and enjoy what God has given us, it is good. If this rather short answer feels unsatisfactory, it is. But do not despair! The remainder of the book explores what God wants for us and who we are in him.

While I believed the freedom God wanted to bring me was real, I had a very hard time trusting him. The Israelites felt the same way. Just as Pharaoh suggested the wilderness would shut the Israelites in (Exodus 14:3-4), I felt shut in, not able to trust the freedom in front of me.

Let's look at their story of exodus from Egypt. When Pharaoh finally came to his senses and realized he had released his free workforce (i.e., slaves), he rallied all his chariots and riders and took off after the Israelites. The Israelites were camped between their enemies and the sea. You can bet they worried where they would be going next, or if Moses had led them out "to be slaughtered because there were not enough graves in Egypt" (Exodus 14:11). God commanded them to not be afraid because he would deliver them out of their enemies' hands, and then his glory would be known in all of Egypt.

I imagine this as a movie, and the cinematography is sweeping. The people are freaking out, Moses is reminding them God will fight for them, and God is telling Moses to keep them moving! He then told Moses to raise his staff, the sea before them splits and forms walls so the people could walk on dry floor of the sea. As this is going on, the angel leading them fell to the back of them, clouding and confusing the Egyptians in darkness but giving the Israelites light to see as they crossed on dry land in the night. In the last watch of the night, Israel was close to crossing, and God threw the army into confusion. He commanded Moses to put his staff down. As his arms came down, the Egyptians were defeated by the crushing waters folding over them. God's glory would be known throughout all of Egypt.

The people were in awe of what God had done! Who wouldn't be! They sang a song of praise, and Miriam, Moses' sister and prophetess, picked up a tambourine, and all the women joined her in song and dance. Three days later...their new reality hit them. They were in the desert, a world of scarcity and worry as they moved further into the wilderness. Where would they sleep? What would they eat and drink? Would they end up back in slavery? There were so many of them. How was Moses going to make sure that all of their needs were met? Moses would not be able to meet the needs, but God, with his grace and provision could.

They need not have worried—easier said than done for all of us—God made bitter water sweet and spoke to them, saying, "If you will give earnest heed to the voice of the LORD your God, and do what is right in his sight, and give ear to his commandments, and keep all his statutes, I will put none of the diseases on you which I have put on the Egyptians; for I, the LORD, am your healer" (Exodus 15:26).

God names himself a healer. He is *your* healer. I think about this for the Israelites. I think about this for you and me. Is this not a journey into the wilderness to be healed from our brokenness? Egypt was not working for them anymore. They were oppressed.

God knew it was time for his people to know who he was: the God of Abraham, Isaac, and Jacob. God led the Israelites on dry ground through the Red Sea and crashed the waters onto the Egyptian army as they safely walked to the other side and into the wilderness. They were safe! They had to trust him. There was nowhere else to go.

They were also hungry. They complained about needing food, worried they would die of hunger in the wilderness, and wondering if they should have stayed in Egypt. At least they knew there they could eat. Dramatic much? God spoke to Moses and said he would rain manna down from heaven to eat in the morning and quail to eat in the evening (Exodus 16:4). There were specific rules to gathering the manna, especially on the sixth and seventh day. On the sixth day, they would gather twice as much manna, so that on the seventh day they could rest and not work. Not only did they have to trust God to feed them, they had to trust him to count the days and not forget extra portions. The *Lexham Bible Dictionary* says, "The precise meaning of this Hebrew term is unknown; it may mean 'What is it?' which is what the Israelites said upon first seeing the food."[1] I love that God provides for them in an unexpected way; he created something new for them in the wilderness.

The Israelites complained again later in their journey about not having enough water. They said they and their livestock would die of thirst in the wilderness. They would have been better off in Egypt. Drama llamas, but I think we can relate! Moses cried out to God and told him to strike a rock with his staff, and water would flow from it so the people could drink (Exodus 17:1-7).

God provided manna, then quail, and water. He provided shade with his cloud during the day in the desert and heat at night with his pillar of fire. He showed them the way. He answered them. He listened to Moses; who spoke on the Israelites' behalf. No matter how much God provided or kept them safe, the Israelites entered this cycle. They didn't see or feel God's immediate presence, complained, did something to disobey, received some sort of punishment, and then continued in obedience. Moses intervened on their behalf or on God's behalf, and this obedience, disobedience, and repentance cycle started all over again.

In *The Critical Journey*, Hagberg and Guelich express this well and how a person in this cycle can move forward or stay stuck.

> Ironically, in this stage (1), the very behavior that initially brought people to a recognition of God can become a cage for them. For instance, a grave sense of need. If in recognizing God and beginning the journey we do not accept that God can help answer our needs out of love and care; if we reject God's overtures to us, we can become caged in rigorous self-defeating behavior. If, in our utter awe of God, we do not move toward this source of joy, we can let ourselves become overwhelmed, inadequate, and gradually less worthwhile.[2]

The Israelites saw God's goodness, believed, and turned their hearts towards him. Then they started believing they knew their needs better than their Creator. God gave the Israelites a space to draw closer to him even though they were unsure of what this new relationship would look like. They had to use their awe of God to move forward, or they would get stuck in the wilderness. Spoiler alert: They got stuck in the wilderness.

I did this too and still do. I thought it would be an easy switch from saying yes to all of the things to being more generous with my no's. It would just be a new thing I did. I did not realize that I needed a change in mindset on scarcity, provision, and who gets the glory. I started to loosen my grip on caring about what others thought of me. It was terrifying, and I was worried I would not be able to grow.

I've seen God do many miracles in my life. They always appeared when I felt like I was drowning; whenever the thought of something happening to my security or provision threatened to overwhelm me. If something started to happen, like not having control over financial situations, I would freak-the-freak-out. When we were down to zero, I would always scramble and look for ways that I could make a buck. I felt like the pressure was on me to make sure ramen was at least on the table, and we could cover the bills. Yet, God showed up several times to provide for us—random scholarships, free meals, etc. As we have moved through life, I have come to a place of knowing he's got us.

Perhaps, yes, I can help with things, but I shouldn't let my sanity and "go mode" get in the way of seeing him move. This was one of the first areas that God used to break down my being good. I hid a lot of my past financial worries from my husband, Eric, so he didn't know why I would act so crazy and flustered to get those last couple of dollars and make sure we had something in the account. I was trying to be the best financial caretaker. I wanted to make it look like we were good and taken care of. I wanted to look like we were keeping up with the Jones'. I prided myself on being a MacGyver and Jane-of-all-trades, finding solutions to challenges and not going to God first—waiting on his provision.

Reading and studying about God providing the Israelites food, water, and safety from the Egyptians in the desert helped me take a deep breath. It helped reveal the grip I had on finances and looking the part. I slowly began to gain freedom in taking care of our money without it taking me down. God showed me that I could come to him frustrated and ask him to provide a way before being a zealous money maker—usually in the form of taking on extra freelance work, staying up way too late, keeping me from rest, and being able to keep a straight head on my shoulders. After these new habits were being worked into my life, I was finally able to talk to Eric about my fears. My worrying grip began to loosen on provision and security—I started releasing control to God.

Trusting solely on myself to provide for myself and others is a recipe for disaster. It keeps me trapped in slavery. Doing anything on my own strength leaves me bitter and complaining. It distracts from the glory God should receive, and the joy I could have. If I trust God, I allow him to heal the broken parts of me I know need his love so I can be a person set apart and holy.

What does all of this have to do with being good? I had not realized how consumed I was with keeping up appearances, being good, and pleasing everyone. I began to thank God and praise him, as he showed me how hard I worked to feel fulfilled by pleasing people—putting everyone first and forgetting about myself. He showed me it was okay for my life to not look crazy busy which was one way my life could look different—set apart in a holy way. I HAD NO CHOICE. It was to trust God or melt into my be-good, masked self forever. Being good for everyone and knowing God called me to something better, made my soul ache.

When I trust God, even if I cannot see him—like the Israelites could see his glory in pillars—it allows me to take a step back from my control of life. I think I have control through people-pleasing. This is a lie. I think I can control how I react to situations and how I look from the outside, but eventually, that mask will fail. If I can take a deep breath, see the manna falling from the sky, and say, "What is this?" I can listen to the whisper of God saying, "It's my provision. I've got this. You can release the control to trust me and move forward in your journey. I am here. I am taking care of you. Trust me."

things to think about

I hope and pray God shows up for you
and you can notice how he is moving.

1. Do you feel like you can trust God? Write down a
    time you saw him provide.

2. Do you trust what God says about who you are?

3. Which cycle do you have a harder time navigating?
    Belief and unbelief in God or self-reliance and reli-
    ance on God? Why do you think this?

three

lessons in authentic relationships

I may have been helping out of love, but the root of my helping, was to be loved. I was serving people because I was in need of their gratitude for my fulfillment. I confused this way of life for how I thought Jesus lived his. It was not my best life. It was my best for their life.

As we learn to trust God, the next step in our journey is to evaluate how authentic we are with our community and if we trust them. May we be brave and remove the "be-good" mask for a few trusted souls. It is time to do something a little scary to be genuine with those who trust us and ask them for help, maybe for the first time. Without doing this, we cannot move forward.

I hope to challenge how we think about our authenticity with our people. Think about what you are putting into those relationships. Do they bring you life, or drag you down, as you give them life? Are you sharing with them as they share with you? Are you asking for help and support when you need it? Our communal relationships are not just for giving or receiving but also for healing and helping.

Answering those questions may feel difficult. So, let's start small by thinking about relationships in general. Take a few minutes to think about how honest you are in the different kinds of relationships listed below using those questions as a guide.

[ ] Family – spouses, kids, siblings, parents, and in-laws. I know family can be tricky. Start with those of whom you have a decent relationship.

[ ] Friends – If you are like me, you know many people but only let a few in. Consider Jesus; he had 72 disciples (Luke 10:1-12), the 12 apostles (Luke 9:10), and from the disciples, his three closest friends (Mark 14:33).

[ ] You – yes, you. We are working with all relationships, and that includes the one with yourself. You cannot move forward without looking honestly at yourself, and how you feel and work with you.

[ ] Holy Trinity - Father, Son, and Holy Spirit. Whether you've had a quiet time every day or you just talk to them when you need them. This needs to be examined—please do not skip this one!

I hope this exercise has helped you think about your relationships, how honest you are in them and with yourself, as we move forward in this chapter.

There are a few ways to look at our communities and our authenticity within them. We do not have to share everything with everyone (nor should we), but we do need to take off our be-good mask and learn to share more than just the surface of ourselves.

I'll go first and share two examples of people supporting me and giving me wise advice. These are lessons I learned in taking off my mask, showing more vulnerability, asking for and accepting help. I acted like everything was always okay, good, or fine. I did not ask for anything. Helping others made me feel needed, and it kept me busy. It kept me distracted from my feelings, and the thoughts nagging me to change. I had amazing friends around me. Truly. They loved me well despite me not sharing more about my life and being vulnerable about hurts and needs. They allowed it for a while. Then slowly, one by one, they broke down the barrier.

These two stories made specific marks on my memory because my friends showed up when I did not know I needed it or did not know how to ask for help.

I was pregnant with my second, we were getting ready to move, and Eric was traveling a ton for work. I made a prayer request at our mom's group at church about hoping to get all the things done to stage our home and pack while Eric was traveling. I needed help desperately, but I was afraid to admit it or look like I couldn't do it all. Then the gentle nudge of a friend managed to get me to ask for help. I still remember the day she came over for the first time. I tried to look put together—but I was not. And rightly so (now I know this). I saw her standing on my doorstep with her two littles, ready to help in any way. Her kids played with my oldest. She didn't judge me; instead, she lifted me up in a hard time. This was such a small act of kindness that helped me learn to trust. She loved me for who I was, mess and all. When I was weary, her home was always open for coffee and conversation, and over the years, we fought many battles together.

This next one feels super vulnerable. Eric and I led a small group for a few years. As I struggled with depression and anxiety—I had not let anyone in on it yet—our friends noticed me not sharing during prayer time. I would be vague or say I was stressed, but nothing more. I thought I was covering it well. I thought I had my be-good mask on tight. But as depression loomed, it got harder to pull off "I'm fine" with a smile. My friends did notice because, well, they are my friends! One brave friend voiced how she felt: I knew all the groups junk (weaknesses, trials, and sorrows), but they did not know any of mine. Consequently, they did not know how to support or pray for me. Let me tell you, this conversation hurt. I felt destroyed because my friends felt that I didn't trust them. I saw the truth in that and decided to grow in it.

While I made that decision to trust them, it was a slow burn to opening up to them. It was hard to let go of the shame I held onto for having to ask for help. I was clinging to the false belief that I had to give all of myself to everyone all the time in my own power. Taking this tiny step helped spark a flame in the darkness of that lie.

In Exodus 17, we get to see Moses' perspective. As a leader, he had to set the example for relationships and trusting others. We will see how they supported him and gave him wise counsel.

At the end of Exodus 17, Amalek came to fight Israel. How would Moses lead them? Would they follow? Would they succeed? What would come of it?

Moses asked Joshua (his aide) to hand-pick men he trusted to take them into battle against Amalek. Moses, with two of his friends, Aaron and Hur, went up to a higher place so they could watch the battle. As the battle ensued, Joshua took ground when Moses kept his staff raised. As the fighting continued, Moses got tired. Every time he lowered his staff, Joshua lost ground. So Moses's friends found him a seat and held his arms high for the win(Exodus 17:12). In Exodus it says, "His hands were steady until the sun went down." The men Joshua hand-picked helped him win the battle. Together, all these men trusted each other and defeated the enemy.

Sometimes we need people to literally hold us up and help us witness the miracles (especially the ones that can be hard to see) that God performs in our lives. Can I get an amen? Moses trusted his people to help him, and he trusted Joshua to chose the right people with whom to go into battle.

I find Exodus 18 delightful! It begins with Moses receiving Jethro (his father-in-law), Zipporah (his wife), and his two boys. Moses had sent his family to Jethro either before his journey to Egypt or while in Egypt. There was rejoicing in the camp. Moses told Jethro all the things that God had done! Glory! Jethro rejoiced and praised God for what he had done by offering up a sacrifice with Aaron.

However joyful the news was, Jethro saw the heavy load that Moses was carrying. When their encampment was not on the move, Moses would sit and listen to every problem and attempt to solve it. Jethro saw that this was not good.

> He said to him, "The thing that you are doing is not good. You will surely wear out, both yourself and these people who are with you, for the task is too heavy for you; you cannot do it alone. Now listen to me: I will give you counsel, and God be with you...If you do this thing and God so commands you, then you will be able to endure, and all these people also will go to their place in peace." So Moses listened to his father-in-law and did all that he had said (Exodus 18:17-20, 23-24).

It kind of sounds like Jethro was trying to give good advice to someone "being good" and trying to be everything to everyone. Moses was definitely trying to carry too big a load trying to make sure everyone felt heard, helped, and that they were getting the correct resolution. I will say, we should give him some credit and grace as he's doing a pretty good job for someone who has never led a nation through a wilderness and got hired from a burning bush.

The advice he received from Jethro was in good timing. The people were no longer in crisis trying to flee Egypt. Things had settled down, so much so that Jethro believed it was safe enough to bring the family together. Jethro's advice was wise, and he also encouraged Moses to seek God's counsel on the matter. He knew Moses could not do this alone; it was an incredibly overwhelming job. (Sounds like life?) Jethro guided Moses in his leadership, allowing him to focus on his calling, call others to lead, and do something good for the community. Through the wise assessment of his father-in-law, he learned he must divide the load and share his weaknesses, so he might follow what God had called him to do.

A first step for a people-pleaser is to take a step towards Jesus and a person(s) close to you that you can trust. To do that, you have to take off your be-good mask. This sucks. No one, I repeat, no one likes doing this. The kindness you show yourself in this simple act will allow you to love yourself for who you are and who you were made to be. I can't promise that you will go forth every day with that confidence, but you will have at least seen it and know it is possible.

Let's pause to talk about why we are going to do this hard thing. The be-good, people-pleasing life may look nice and productive; however, what good is a nice productive life if there is no one to share it with? Do you find yourself more honest about your feelings and needs with strangers than those in your immediate circle?

When you look in the mirror, what do you see? Do you see a disappointment, a helper, a good human, a failure, someone who has potential and uniqueness but isn't using it, a child of God, a friend?

When I looked into the mirror, I saw someone who was failing at most things, and in most relationships, because she kept saying yes to all the things. For example, I thought a good girl should say yes to:

- Help friends with anything
- Volunteering at church and filling in all of the gaps
- Play-dates
- Running a business and doing all of it
- A clean and perfect household
- Organic (when you can afford it) and wholesome meals
- Making sure your kids don't have too much screen-time
- Hanging out with all your friends; all the time

I do realize most of these are geared towards moms—stay-at-home moms for that matter—but take some time to name the "shoulds" you think you are supposed to do.

A fundamental element of the people-pleasing life is not letting anyone in. Not only was I great at hiding feelings from friends, family, and especially my husband, I also hid my feelings from God. Which is ridiculous because you can't hide from God, we just choose not to be honest with him.

I am by no means a perfect friend, and I know now that my friends also do not want a perfect friend. Taking steps toward Jesus, for me, looked like learning to love them better as I learn what they need, not just by assuming I know what they need. When we look at Jesus' life, we see that he already knew the stories of the people he was helping, yet he took the time to ask questions and listen.

I am grateful for the Holy Spirit who leads me to say something or to shut my mouth and listen. I thank God for the friends who have stuck around as I have journeyed through sharing my whole self. Friends, I thank you for sticking around. Friends help friends. Friends carry friends. Friends laugh, cry, and fight for each other. When they look like they are drowning, friends speak truth or just hold them. I also need to listen to their wise counsel. In the end, I hope you will learn to love yourself for who God says you are (remember our intro, he is pleased with you before you do anything) and the good work you were called to (which we are always moving towards). I cannot promise you will go forth every day with that confidence, but I hope you have a pulse on it and know it is possible.

God has done a good work in my life since I began this journey—physically, mentally, emotionally, and spiritually. We will have moments of fear, but we've got this. You've got this. God has you. Don't do this alone. Find a small group of friends to help you face your weaknesses and journey through the wilderness to the promised land. Without our community, we cannot move forward. Let us not wander another moment alone!

things to think about

*I hope and pray God shows up for you
and you can notice how he is moving.*

1. Can you ask for help and then allow the help to happen?

2. How will you choose what to share with people you trust?

3. Is there a person who has told you what you are doing is not good? Was it wise council? Did it bring about change?

4. What "shoulds" do you have in your life that you might need to examine?

5. Can you name a person you are willing to start this journey with?

four

how Jesus related to others

I must be honest with you about something. As we know, I grew up in a Christian home, attending church, serving, having quiet times, and checking all the boxes. There were many times I would study, read, and explore, but I would almost always avoid the stories of Jesus. I did not really notice this until one day, when I was standing in the aisles of a Christian bookstore looking at what kind of Bible study I could get next. It was an in-between time when nothing was going on at church. I needed a book to help me study because I struggled to concentrate when I read the Bible. I had done nearly every Beth Moore study, so her independent study books drew me in, but they were thick and intimidating books: *90 Days with Paul, 90 Days with David, and 90 Days with Jesus.* Very quickly, I chose not to study Jesus. This almost reflexive choice caused me to pause for a minute—what made me not want to examine Jesus, my Savior, whom I am supposed to emulate and be like and be loved by? He was the whole reason why I do all the things, isn't he?

I believe I was too scared to study Jesus because that meant I would draw him near to my worries, the darkness I was feeling, and this was too vulnerable. I chose Paul (and later David) because he was less scary. I would rather study the two guys I knew had messed up and weren't perfect instead of studying my Jesus. So, if you have trepidations about diving into Jesus (which is what we are about to do), know that you are not alone.

As we enter this chapter, I encourage you to look at your story and move out of your people-pleasing, "be-good" era. We will do this by stepping into the New Testament to examine how Jesus carried out human life as fully God and fully man. My hope is you will see Jesus pointing us to a better way.

I will share the stories of Jesus to show us hope. Why do we have hope? Why do we need hope? Because he came, lived, died, was raised to life, ascended to heaven, and left us the Holy Spirit, who guides and directs us not physically with clouds and a pillar of fire—like he did for the Israelites—but from within our beloved bodies. We need hope to make it through this people-pleasing journey to be free, giving glory to God—just like Jesus did.

As we explore the stories from the Gospels, let's look and see if Jesus tells us to be good.

There were 400 years of silence between the pages of the Old Testament and New Testament. God was still there, but he pulled away from speaking to the masses through the prophets. The role of a prophet was usually a formal one. They would speak or act with inspiration and direction from God to proclaim his will. For example, Isaiah warned Israel of God's judgment against them if they did not repent and turn from their rebellious ways (Isaiah 1-39). When we pick up the story in the New Testament, God's people were under oppressive rule first under the Ptolemies of Egypt then the Roman Empire. One can see why the Jewish people were begging God to come down and save them.

God saw and heard them. It was time to act and send Jesus, the better Moses (Hebrews 3:3), and the ultimate leader through all wilderness. In the first chapters of the Gospels of Matthew and Luke, we are introduced to the promise of Jesus' coming. Mary learned from an angel that she would conceive him through the Holy Spirit. She went to see her cousin, Elizabeth, who was also pregnant with John (who would become known as John the Baptist). John jumped inside Elizabeth's womb when he heard Mary's voice. Elizabeth exclaimed that Mary was blessed because she believed what God said he would do (Luke 1:42). After Jesus was born, she and Joseph visited the temple to fulfill their customs. We know God ordained this time because Simeon and Anna had been promised they would see the Messiah (the promised savior and deliverer the Israelites anticipated in the OT) before they died, and they were waiting in the temple (Luke 2:25-40).

Soon Herod, the king of Judea, was informed by traveling Magi of a new king's birth. Herod grew jealous and issued a decree to kill all the boys under two years old. Joseph, Mary, and Jesus fled to Egypt. When Herod died, Joseph had a dream that it was safe to return (Matthew 2).

It's fascinating how the beginning of Jesus' life parallels Moses' life. Both were born during 400 years of being ruled by a series of ruthless leaders. The leaders at the time had glory and power at the expense of the people—like wanting to kill all the boys of Israel in Egypt or all the boys under two in Bethlehem.

Now, this might be reading into the stories a bit, but when something new is coming, it means the death of something else. Where do you see that something needs to die in your life that you may live a new, more fulfilling life?

After growing up as normal as he could as the God-man, Jesus began his ministry. First, he had to prepare for the journey. John the Baptist, the baby who leapt in Elizabeth's womb, grew up to be the one who paved the way for Jesus's ministry. And when John baptized Jesus, it marked the virtual end of John's ministry and the beginning of Jesus's (Matthew 3). When Jesus was baptized, the Holy Spirit descended from heaven, and God said, "This is my Son, whom I love; with him I am well pleased" (Matthew 3:17).

Can we note that Jesus had done nothing except be born, grow, study, and live? No ministry or miracles, and no disciples had been called. The Father was just pleased with the Son. What a beautiful image for us to hold.

I love the connection to the Israelites in what happens next. The Israelites were led into the wilderness for 40 years after crossing the Red Sea because they did not trust God, and the Spirit led Jesus into the wilderness for 40 days after being baptized to show us how to trust God (Matthew 4:1-11, Luke 4). You may be asking, "Why did the Spirit lead Jesus into the wilderness?" The Israelites went into the wilderness to learn how to be a holy people set apart people, and Jesus went into the wilderness to be tempted by the devil. Scripture tells us Jesus was hungry (fully human) after 40 days of fasting in the wilderness when Satan addressed him as the Son of God (fully God) with a series of questions and temptations. Jesus shows us how to walk through challenging times by trusting God for—provision, security, and glory. The Israelites walked into the wilderness via the Red Sea led by a visible God as a pillar of cloud and fire. God showed them his glory and provided all they would need on their journey—food, water, and safety.

Each time Satan approached Jesus, he tried to get Jesus to question his identity. Jesus responded with truth from Scripture, corrected, and challenged Satan when he pulled Scripture out of context. He tried to get Jesus to turn rocks into bread to be his own provider. He tried to get Jesus to test his security by telling him to jump from the mountain, so the angels would catch him. Satan offered Jesus all the kingdoms of the world if he worshiped him. Jesus commanded Satan to leave him, and he finally did. The angels came and provided all that Jesus needed, giving him rest and nourishment at the end of the challenge. Jesus was secure in his identity as Lord despite the human challenges.

While our challenges may not be as clear-cut as Jesus', he sets the example for us of how to approach Satan, others, or even ourselves when we fall into unhealthy patterns. He shows us the importance of knowing scripture. Jesus quoted from Deuteronomy. He would have memorized the Torah (the first five books of the Bible) by the time he was twelve as was custom for Jewish boys. We need to know the truth of God's word. I have felt God walking alongside me in my own challenges, and he has helped guide and remind me of his word which helps me in my obedience.

Scripture was rooted in Jesus' identity. He knew who he was and what he was there for, so he knew that Satan was trying to mess him up. Like Jesus, we have to know who we are. As I felt myself wandering into this wilderness of shedding my people-pleasing layers, I had to be open to the idea of who I was. Once I learned to be open to my true identity, I had to remain rooted in it.

Jesus gives us the tools and shows us how to use them when we are being tempted or struggling. Here are four things we can apply to our lives when we are learning to trust God and walk in obedience:

1. Listen to the Holy Spirit.
2. Know the Word.
3. Believe and trust the Word.
4. Know God will provide, even when it looks different than we thought.

Knowing that Jesus went through this testing and refining and came out on the other side gives me hope. I pray it does the same for you.

In chapter three, we explored community. Here's a joke you may have heard: The biggest miracle Jesus did was having friends over 30! While it is funny, I think it's so relatable for so many people. How did Jesus show authenticity in community? Luke 5 shares the story when Jesus called his first disciples. One particular day, after starting his ministry, he felt the crowd, well, crowding him. He saw Peter and Andrew in their boat and asked if he could use it to move out into the water to speak to the crowd.

First, Jesus asked for help in a small way. Any size ask is okay, but I think we need this reminder that we can start small, too. After he finished teaching, he helped Peter and Andrew with the biggest catch of their lives. They caught so many fish that it broke the nets, and their fishing partners, James and John, had to come help. When they brought their boats to land, Jesus asked them to follow him, and they did so immediately leaving everything behind.

Jesus called his disciples to come and follow him—that's risky business, especially when you have a family and/or a job. Why would one take the risk to follow him? Why was Jesus calling all these people to follow him? The fully-human Jesus also needed community like the fully-God aspect of him had with the Trinity. He was also preparing them by showing them the way to live, teach, and experience his love before they went out and shared his love with the world. For he knew he would not be physically on earth forever.

Later in the Gospel of Luke, as Jesus calls the rest of his disciples, we see a variety of characters. A tax collector, a traitor, a questioner, those who wanted to be first, and they are all beloved by him. If you go and read, you'll notice that he calls them by name. He knew them, everything about them, and he still called them to follow. Even Judas, the one who would betray him, he called him to follow. He showed them so much more of who he was—his compassion, love, grace, mercy, power, anger, and sadness. Jesus had the same emotions we have daily. We will look at specific stories as he interacted with more friends, like Mary, Martha, and Lazarus, throughout our journey. For now, it is good for us to remember that Jesus shows us the good, joyful, annoying, and sad parts of being in community as he walked this Earth.

Since this is a book about people-pleasing, as we walk through the first 30-ish years of Jesus' life, we should ask ourselves, did Jesus show himself to be a people-pleaser? No. In fact, we learn the Father was pleased with him for just showing up, listening and obeying to his earthly parents, and living a quiet life. We do not see aspects of "being good" but rather him knowing and trusting his identity and calling.

As I was wrap up this chapter, I long to give you examples of how I took what Jesus and the Israelites were showing me and immediately put it into action. (There may be a hint of people-pleasing in that statement.) I was struggling to find examples. That's when I realized...I couldn't. I was still learning to see God through a different perspective. I needed to understand what it meant to pay attention to his provision and security. Unfortunately, we don't always get the immediate results of lessons; they take time. I think if I could do it right away, I wouldn't be writing this book or have a relatable story. You'll see those stories throughout this book—sometimes years it took for me to see and recognize God as I moved through the wilderness. I just want to be honest and say I knew I needed to find hope in God, but I just couldn't see it yet.

Walking the line of being good for everyone and knowing God called me to something better did get intense. I did not quite know how to express and understand this tug of war in my soul. I asked my community to pray for me. I learned to ask for help from God when my soul ached, asking him to make change possible and hopeful. I wanted to see a change in my thoughts and my actual life. I wanted others to notice it. This longing made the journey of risks I began to take more glorious as I got to where I am today.

So far we have journeyed alongside Moses and Jesus. Then we looked at Jesus' baptism, God was pleased with him, and why Jesus went into the wilderness. We talked about Jesus trusting in God the Father but also learned how to stand against the devil, our enemy. Next we saw Jesus calling the disciples and how the beginning of his friendship with them started with asking for help. He called them by name and listened to them.

I am slowly learning it is not just what I say and do that God cares about. He cares for my soul; he cares for your soul. He wants us to have freedom from pleasing others, to be free of the demands of the "should." He began a good work in me by revealing that my motivations were going to be part of my soul work. I was all about what others could see, and in my legalistic religion, not knowing I was in for a big surprise of how much God longs for a deep relationship with me and how much he really does care for my soul.

As we learn to shed the layers of our people-pleasing, let's have honest conversations with friends, open our hearts to the Holy Spirit as we step into the wilderness, and let the Father know we are willing to trust him on this journey.

things to think about

I hope and pray God shows up for you
and you can notice how he is moving.

1. Do you trust God to provide what you need?
   Why or why not?

2. Who are the people around you that you can
   ask for help?

3. Is it hard for you to form deep relationships?
   Think about why. Is it an issue with fear,
   trust, or something else?

Part Two

Do Good. How We Relate to Ourselves

five

it's time you have a chat with yourself

I did part-time freelance work after we had our first baby. However, loyalty and no boundaries with the client started to drain
me, my relationship with Eric, and my relationship with our
daughter. I felt lost without work. I thought I had to contribute
financially for security. I loved what I did, but pleasing the client
and wanting extra cash, was taking up too much mental space
and causing me anxiety. This was the first time I started to realize
I was idolizing work.

I stopped freelancing for some time during this transition
from being good to doing good. Now, instead of filling my time
with work, I filled up the space with volunteering at church.
Guess what?! I had a hard time with boundaries there too.
I could not say "no" to all of these good things! It was church

after all, and doesn't Jesus want us to put the gospel first? That's how I justified saying "yes" to all of it.

I made a conscious effort to pray and pay attention as I read scripture to see if anything was being revealed to me. I was impatient. I needed to take time to examine my relationship with God. I had done it in other relationships, and they welcomed it! Trusting God with everything, as in an intimate relationship, felt scary. He is omnipotent (a fancy word for he knows everything) and already knows my struggles. It feels different when there is an option to bring them to him and trust him with them. But if he is my God, and I knew he should be the most important relationship, what was holding me back?

As we begin the journey through the wilderness, paying attention to how we are people-pleasing and the different motivations or reasons for doing so, we will see a shift in doing good. I tried to be more selective with what I said yes to. What does it look like to be doing good on the outside but still ignoring that inner work that truly brings change? It meant still having a hyper-focus on caring too much about my choices and then spiraling into worrying about what people thought of these new choices. I became so devoted to walking away from being good and wanted only to do good that it became an obsession. It brought me to my knees and a conversation with God about why these good things still felt the same.

As I reflect on this time, I wanted so badly to be needed. I always had this vision of what my dream job could be. It was serving alongside someone in the shadows, behind the curtain, moving things without being seen. I wanted to do all the work and not get credit for it, but I would know how much work I did. I didn't think I was cut out for the leading role because everything I had tried so far didn't fit with how I thought life was supposed to go. (I see self-esteem, false humility, and lack of confidence in God as issues that were major catalysts for my depression and anxiety.)

Eventually, we needed some extra money, so I sought a freelance job with a nonprofit I loved. I thought it would be a great mash-up of what I did, but with someone managing my work-load, so I wouldn't overextend myself. Turns out they wanted a lot more than what I could give of myself. But, I wanted to do it! It would be beneficial for my career, and I knew the work we would be doing was good for the community, but I just couldn't. I felt God saying, "It's okay to let this go." I did not want to. I put it off to the point that I felt physically sick. Finally, I called and said I needed to step down—I hadn't known that my client was on vacation; that felt even worse. He was sad because he really thought this would be a great thing and last for a long time. I said I was sorry and felt a huge amount of guilt and shame for quitting. While I had learned about boundaries in the physical, I had still not done the inner work of putting up emotional and spiritual boundaries for myself.

During that time, Eric and I signed up to go to Burundi, Africa, with a non-profit we supported. Homecare is an organization whose goal is to share the hope of Christ with the people of Burundi and see the country restored by partnering with local Burundian Christian leaders. The center and leaders provide the resources to bring hope and help to the people in Burundi. Primarily benefiting widows and orphans, they bring a holistic approach by providing a spiritual connection to Jesus, food, clean water, counseling, literacy, training in trade, business skills, agriculture, and microloans. I called it a mission trip at the time, but when I returned, I claimed it as a vision trip!

This trip opened our eyes to the brokenness of the world. We saw how when power is shared equally, it is beautiful, and God gets the glory. We did not go to do anything. We went to listen to the stories of the Burundian women and learn from those in the program. Women who needed Jesus and physical, spiritual, and emotional help. Oh, they found him! Not help from those of us visiting, but from those serving them day in and day out. Not in the money we sent, but in those loving them, feeding them, and teaching them every day. Those who were being Jesus to them.

I learned to weep with those who weep. I heard stories of deep pain that included things I could not ever imagine happening to a human. I learned to dance with those who dance. I could not believe what they had gone through with such strength. They were able to move from incredible darkness into the brilliant light of Jesus. They were able to forgive with extreme joy and love. They showed me God is good. I learned how to lean on him because of their faith. It was something I desperately needed. This was the start of exploring my inner self.

The vision was caught. "We all have different stories, but the same pain," said best by Peace, the founder of Homecare. The trip truly transformed my perception of myself and who I was in Christ. But I ended up taking that confidence a bit too far. There's no easy way to say how much I cared about what I believed people thought of me. What I thought they believed of me was all in my head. My perception of what people thought of me was that they cared so much about what I did. I had a false confidence that the good work I was doing was showing off God. What I ended up doing was building an idol of false confidence.

I thought I had figured it out! Now I was going to serve on my own terms not based on what others thought I had to do! I intended to serve in all areas of life. So, the most logical thing was to do all the things like Jesus—turned out this is not how he moved about here on Earth. I assumed I would be in step with Jesus. I pressed in too much. I set a strict rule of doing good in the church, community, and at work. It took all my time and energy.

It was impossible to be this new me.

Eric was traveling a lot for work during this time. I tried to stay busy because I missed him, and we had two kids under the age of three. I was afraid to stop, to sit, and think too much about what was happening. I refused to be still. I had to keep going, keep moving. I saw the pattern emerging again. If I stopped, I would break.

Shall we enter back into the story of the Israelites? We are covering a lot of chapters in Exodus (Exodus 20-31), but it equates to 40+ days of their time. An overarching idea is that God was in the Israelites story showing Israel how they could be a people set apart. He named things the cultures around them struggled with and how they could choose to be a light and a blessing by following his laws. When left to their own devices, the Israelites wanted to show devotion and worship something—it didn't always end up being God. It is understandable that they didn't know how to be still and wait. For the first time in forever, they did not have to wake up and fulfill someone else's agenda. How would they know how to have peace and be still?

Israel moved further in the desert, and they arrived at Mount Sinai. They set up camp and God asked to meet with them. He asked them to wash their clothes and be set apart for three days. On the third day, God brought his presence down in thunder and showed himself through flame and smoke on the mountain. The community heard the voice of God as he gave the Ten Commandments. The people were afraid, and they asked Moses to go back up the mountain and speak to God. The Israelites would listen to whatever he said when he came back down.

Moses came down the mountain after listening to God for the new ways for them to live. He told Israel what God told him, and they built an altar to enter into a covenant (a binding agreement) with God. They agreed to do all he said!

God asked Moses to bring Aaron, Joshua, and 72 priests to meet and dine with him (Exodus 24:9-11). Go read this passage; it is a little mind-blowing. It was like a celebration of the covenant and gave those who would be leading the Israelites an interaction with God. After dinner, Moses and his assistant Joshua went up the mountain for 40 days and 40 nights to receive the commandments and laws in stone so that Moses could teach them. When God was done with those instructions, he described a space for him to dwell in among Israel. His glory was too much for them, so he created a plan for the Tabernacle—a place for God to dwell among them.

Meanwhile, the Israelites sat at the base of Mount Sinai waiting as Moses talked to God. Instead of Israel praying to God or calling out to him (because his presence is right there on the mountain), they had a mob mentality and coerced Aaron to make a god for them. Forty days was a long time for Moses to be gone, and they were done waiting. They even said, "We do not know what has become of him" (Exodus 32:1). Everyone brought all the gold they plundered from the Egyptians and made a golden calf. The next day, they brought the golden calf offerings and feasted. Friends, it was just a few days earlier that they had entered a covenant, and now, they had already broken three of the commandments given. While this feels shocking, I can imagine it happening because my heart can swing all in for God one day and all in for me the next day. Thank God for grace.

As Joshua and Moses came down the mountain, they were confused by the noises coming from the camp. Moses saw what was happening, was pissed, and threw the stone tablets. Poor Moses had no idea what was going on. God let him know what was happening, and that he was ready to consume them and make a nation out of Moses instead. Moses asked God not to.

He told God of the glory God would lose because everyone would wonder why he would save them from Egypt but not from themselves. The Lord relented.

Sidenote: The fact that God was angry and Moses talked him out of—it's wild to me—I do not understand it. There are lots of things I don't pretend to be smart enough to get. I hope that this is God showing us that we can intercede for people, especially through prayer. We know that Jesus does it for us, too.

I had created an idol of my work. I put work above all else. God asks to be first; in the OT, he commands to be first. He was not, and my heart and soul needed to reorder the things of importance. Changing my motivation from people-pleasing to becoming set apart by doing his good work would take God and me working together. As I strived to keep up my outward appearance, the Lord looked at my heart and said, *Let's do some work—together.* Three topics in these chapters (Exodus 20-31) have been a big part of my inner work over the years. I was compelled and longed to be set apart, just like the Israelites. I tried everything I could to make my life look holy, and I mostly succeeded. On my own, it was exhausting and not what God had planned. Inner work had to be done.

The three things God brought to my soul's attention were idolatry, identity, and rest. And while these things were specific to me, I do think they apply to most of us people-pleasers (and humans in the twenty-first century). What are we putting in front of God? Who is telling us who we are? Do we know how to rest?

These are patterns you will see mentioned throughout the rest of our journey. They are a bit of a thorn in my soul; things that do not go away but just fade into the background. To be honest, I hate that these are the things I need to continually work on. Maybe you can relate?

Idolatry *(Exodus 20:1-7; 24:9-11)*

Despite Aaron, Aaron's sons, and the elders seeing God and communing with him, they allowed the Israelites to renounce their commitment to God. They helped Israel build an idol and even blamed the people when Moses came back down. This short time frame gave me both despair and hope. I thought, oh, how quickly they forgot! At the same time, I know how dismissive of his presence I can be just moments after I have spent time with God, or he has blessed me or given me direction.

Idolatry during my recovery time as a people-pleaser caused me not to respect my boundaries, worry about all the things, and not give up control. I confused loyalty and devotion to people and things as serving God when, really, I had put these things above my relationship with God.

Identity *(Exodus 31:1-11)*

God gave Moses instructions for the Tabernacle. He revealed that there are specific people to do this beautiful work. He instilled in them the wisdom, knowledge, and gifts for creating the entire Tabernacle and leading the others who would help them.

I don't know about you, but when in the wilderness, I do not feel equipped to create or lead. In fact, at this stage of my leaving a be-good life, I felt ill-equipped and overwhelmed by everything I had said yes to. I had overpromised and was stretched thin. I didn't think I could build anything beautiful. I didn't believe God could be for me, or that he could fill me with his presence to make something beautiful for his glory. I thought I had failed. I did not believe what I knew to be true about me.

Rest *(Exodus 20:8; 31:12-18)*

Boundaries were something I needed to learn how to build. The idea of being still made me worry I was being lazy. I can't even describe how much I did not want to believe that rest was good or biblical. Over the last decade, God has taught me a lot about learning to rest, showing me what a blessing it is to me and to him.

Thank God. He saw me falling hard as I worked to feel fulfilled by pleasing people. God is really good at revealing how we can draw closer to him. We just have to pay attention. In Exodus, he showed the Israelites how to be set apart with the Ten Commandments and the other laws and ordinances, which were on repeat, throughout the Old Testament. Israel went through cycles of idolatry, being where they shouldn't, and not believing their identity as children of God—a people set apart and holy.

Being set apart, believing our true identity, and learning to find true rest is possible to attain with God! We can be a light, a people set apart, but first we may have to let God burn our idols to the ground—anything we set as more important than

God, even if it looks good or is well-meaning. When I say we should let him burn it down, it is not in a negative, bad guy, bully sense. We have the choice every day to say yes or no. I didn't like what he wanted me to burn down, though. It always came in the form of pride.

My pride needed to be torn down and rebuilt to understand humility. It is not that I was holding things over people and lording that I was the best. I did a great job of serving, but it was my heart. Man looks at the outward, but the Lord looks at the heart. Ugh. The fulfillment I found in being good for others, helping them out, putting everyone first and forgetting about me—this was pride. This was me soaking up that I knew I was being good by serving God and others but also filling my heart with pride. Always being everything to everyone is what drove me.

God was there, and he still showed up, despite me not always recognizing him as the one guiding me to do what he asked me to do. Ultimately, it was my decision (he does give us free will), but I believe God asked me to say no to these things:

- Placing a higher value on work and relationships than him
- Believing my identity is in what I produce
- Giving all of myself to the point of exhaustion

I said, "Okay, I trust you" and walked away. It felt so good and free! That does not mean it was not incredibly difficult to do.

I burned some bridges, hurt feelings, and broke agreements. I needed those "yeses" to be where I am today, but I'm so thankful I decided to turn them into "nos."

As I wrap up with a scrappy bow, I encourage you to read or listen to Exodus 20-32. In those chapters you will find how God wanted to help shape and form the Israelites into a people set apart—giving them laws to help seek justice and instruction for the Tabernacle to see beauty and awe when they worshiped him.

things to think about

I hope and pray God shows up for you
and you can notice how he is moving.

1. Do I care too much about what people think of me, my actions, or my words?

2. What patterns in my inner life do I see as I read the scriptures?

3. What motivates me?

4. What does God want me to burn down?

six

i'm fine, everything is fine, except that it's not

If you or someone you know struggles with mental health and needs help, in the USA you can call or text 988 24 hours a day, seven days a week for free and confidential support. If you think you need help, call your doctor or start with a trusted friend. Those first steps are hard. It is okay to ask for help. You matter. We need you. Stick around.

I am not a doctor. I am simply here to tell my story about depression and anxiety. I am grateful to say that thanks to medication, friends, Jesus, and the Word of God, I am here to share it.

This chapter is about the undercurrent of things going on inside me for as long as I can remember. So, this would be a good time to point out that this book isn't entirely a chronological account of my story. Most of it is, but the inner work of Part Two is woven throughout my story and continues to be.

When I was recognizing character qualities that needed to grow I started to slow down. Slowing down caused me to sit and think. Sitting and thinking caused my thoughts to spiral, like the spiraling storm of *If You Give a Mouse a Cookie*. Except, in this case, the mouse is a busy, people-pleasing person, and the cookie is silence. This spiral is not as fun as Mr. Mouse makes it look.

I grew up in a time and place (the 1990s) where depression and anxiety were hidden. Mental health was not talked about. If you had such illnesses, you lived with that darkness in secret. If it was found out, some might say your faith had faltered or you were living in sin. One of my spiritual gifts is faith. So, I can tell you that I kept my mouth shut when I felt sad, overwhelmed, or anything negative. I did not have words for depression and anxiety.

Sidenote: I want to pause and speak to those around you that may be saying what you are going through is only because of spiritual warfare. I'd like to say, maybe. Sometimes we over-spiritualize, sometimes we don't take our health seriously. Just because I am depressed does not mean I am not spiritual enough. It can be a chemical imbalance—it can have to do with my environment and how God is using it to help me change my mindset or begin to lean into him and my community. Maybe we start thinking about getting healthy both mentally and spiritually.

I remember my first panic attacks in college. I thought I was just overreacting or too emotional. I had two in very public places. I was filled with shame and fear after those happened. I did not understand it was my body telling me something was going on. That something was wrong. I was not okay. As I look back at my story and remember, I can see now that most of these panic attacks were happening around my next steps. What job would I take after college? Would people think highly of me? Is this what I want to do for the rest of my life? The questions and doubts circled identity and security.

One thing I was confident in was marrying Eric. We got married right after I graduated—like the day after. We then attended grad school (for two very different things— graphic design and geology). I got pregnant with our first daughter, Ella, while we were finishing school. Eric interviewed for the job he still has today while at the hospital the day after Ella was born. Funnily enough, our second daughter, Mia, came 18 months later—and we signed the papers to buy our first home in the hospital after I had her. Life took off quickly from there.

In 2015, the girls went to a preschool program, and the depression—I wasn't aware I had—grew deeper and darker. I kept feeling off. It got worse as I was at home with two kids under two, and Eric traveled for weeks on end for work. Eventually, we enrolled the girls in a pre-k program so I could get part-time work and run errands. After I dropped the girls off, I would have moments of extreme productivity, and then I would sit and stare out the window. Not in a good, wistful, and dreamy way, but in a frozen, didn't know what to do or want to move kind of way. I did not like being alone. It made me think about all the emotions I had stuffed down. I continued to fill my time with saying yes and promising above and beyond.

I was clearly exhausted, running myself into the ground, becoming more irritable, not sleeping, and worried about everything. I got to the point where I would drop the girls off at preschool, go home, and just cry. I felt so sad, and I could not figure out why. I felt like a failure and a phony. My mask was crumbling, and I didn't know what to do.

I was saying everything was fine at Bible study and with friends. My ability to be authentic in this area was close to zero (Chapter 3). There were so many times that I wanted to say more than, "I'm fine" or "It's going good." They weren't always lies but it didn't feel like the truth. I struggled to find the words to shout, "I need help!" I also struggled to have a prayer request for myself instead of all the other people in my life. I over-spiritualized and thought this might be happening because I was not doing enough good for God or not reading the Bible enough. That, I realize, was my legalistic past speaking. The truth was I was struggling with depression and anxiety. Thankfully, God had arranged a time, as he does, to gently help me realize I needed help.

Not that I think life must be fair, but I do think that if I am going to ask you to take time to examine your life and soul, I'll have to go first. Here we go.

Feeling overwhelmed.

I couldn't function. I would drop the girls off at daycare or preschool, or they'd nap. I'd have a laundry list of things to do, but I did not know where to start. It was all overwhelming. I thought I had to be the perfect mom, wife, friend, and human. The items on the list were things I could do, but I was paralyzed.

Fear of being alone.

Security is a big issue for me. Not safety in the physical sense, but the fear of something happening to my husband. I would spiral in thoughts when Eric would travel—thinking something would happen to him or...who knows what. I would end up on the floor, sitting and crying, surrounded by laundry and not knowing what to do. I would be overwhelmed and paralyzed, again.

Sadness.

Other times I would just be really sad. I wanted everything to stop. I didn't want to be needed for a week. I didn't want to have things to do for a couple of weeks. It felt very selfish, so I would cry for a bit and then do something to keep the sadness away.

These feelings—feeling overwhelmed, fear of being alone, and sadness—would only happen when the house was quiet. I would normally have friends over or be out doing stuff. So, it didn't happen much, but it did start to happen more frequently. The thoughts and conversations would begin to swirl around in my brain and be all muddled. It looked and sounded like intense pressure in my head. So many times I wished I had a valve that could release the pressure of all these thoughts and opinions and negative things.

I started to worry when I couldn't calm the voices in my head. I had always been able to stuff things down, but now it was all the time. So much so, that I wasn't sleeping. I had to blast music to be able to focus. I believed I was not good enough. I was not enough. I could never be enough. Those moments scared me. That's when, in my darkest, I knew I had to talk to someone and ask for help. It had now been over a year of this intensity.

I was able to attend the IF:Gathering (a Christian conference) that spring. At the event, a speaker shared a story about herself or her mom, I do not remember the exact details, but I do remember the story being incredibly profound. It was the first time I had heard someone talk about depression from the stage, and all the feelings she shared were exactly what I was going through.

I finally felt seen. My pain felt named. The shame felt like it could be lifted. Maybe. It was the first time I felt hope in a long time. I went home from IF and thought about what the speaker had said. I continued to read the Bible even though it felt like it was not doing me any good. Eventually, God spoke. He told me I had been at this mountain long enough (Deuteronomy 2). It was time to move on. I cried out, *How!?* I would only move on with him guiding the way.

He guided me by bringing to mind a doctor I felt with whom I could have a safe conversation. I was hesitant to contact her. I reached out and asked for help. I felt spiritually weak and ashamed for needing help. I never thought a good Christian girl like me would ever have to take medication. Depending on when and where you grew up, and if you were in a Christian space, you may have been taught that people shouldn't need medication for things like depression and anxiety. We were told, "Perhaps you need to pray more," or "There is a sin in your life you need to repent from," or "We have victory in Jesus, so we don't need medication!" If you had depression and anxiety, you probably also carried the heavy load of shame and guilt. I know now not all mental illness is a spiritual attack. Our bodies are broken, and sometimes, we need help (for our entire lives or a certain period of it) from the smart doctors to whom God gave wisdom.

After I began taking medication, God guided me again and reminded me of the story from IF. So I started talking to a very small group of friends about what I was going through. We established a texting rhythm. I would text them on hard days so they could pray for me. I had to respond with how I was actually doing if they checked in on me. I finally didn't feel alone in my darkness.

I had to untangle so many lies from the enemy (Satan). They were little twists in the truth. The Israelites had lies they had to untangle as well. Exodus 32 is all about the consequences of their actions. They broke the covenant with God, and as a result, there was death and chaos after the golden calf incident. The Lord said it was time to move on without him, and he would send an angel in his place. Moses, gosh, I'm glad he was bold, said he wouldn't move forward without God. He said that they needed his presence, and that he needed God's presence to lead these stiff-necked people.

As Moses recounted their story to them, I wonder if he felt alone and depressed or if the Israelites felt anxious? Did they feel that way even though they could see God's presence? I wonder if they experienced a bit of the dark night of the soul. Then God said he would go with them. Yes! Then, in an even bolder move, Moses asked to see God's glory. God told Moses to stand in the cleft of the mountain, and he would let him see a glimpse of his goodness and glory. For if he saw it all, he would not survive. Moses saw and then got back to work. He brought the second set of the 10 Commandment tablets, building instructions for the Tabernacle, and a list of names to help lead the building and crafting down the mountain, and his face shone because he had been in God's presence. This scared the people, so he would wear a veil while speaking to them until he went into God's presence again (Exodus 34-39).

At the end of the book, God came near (Exodus 40:34-37). They built the Tabernacle—a dwelling place for God's glory— so that he could be among them when they moved from this mountain to the next place God directed them. This would be how God would lead them through the wilderness. When his glory, like a cloud, filled the tabernacle, no one could come near, and they knew to stay. When it lifted, they knew it was time to move camp.

When Moses begged God to come with him in Exodus 33, that's how I felt. I thought God had left me, that his presence was no longer near to me because I was covered in darkness. I know he hadn't actually left me, but it felt like it. Hope felt lost.

Your mountains may be different than mine and the Israelites. They might come in different forms. The foothills of my mountains were security and provision. The Great Rockies were depression and anxiety. Much like all the questions that the Israelites asked, I asked God why I was feeling so dark. I avoided time by myself because I became immobile when I was in silence. I couldn't move. I couldn't do anything. I also didn't know how to talk to anyone about what was going on let alone be able to have an honest conversation with God! Moses showed me that God was not afraid of me, my thoughts, my questions. More than anything, he wanted me to feel like I had an honest, open relationship with him. Moses opened the door to helping me feel courageous to talk to God honestly, and Jesus showed me how to do that.

What is the point of these mountains? It was not to simply look at them and know that I was going to hike over them and dominate them. After crying and pleading asking God to take away my pain—this weakness—he said, *No*. I was mad. But then I started to understand what I really could do with the knowledge of living with depression and anxiety. Truth be told, I had been living with them for a very long time; I just didn't know it. Now I was free. Why? Because I knew how to name the things that were bringing me to tears or paralysis or anger. These were the thorns in my side.

Now I have great hours, days, weeks, maybe a month. Then, sometimes, I have bad hours, days, weeks, or months. I know how to cope with them. I have brought certain people closer.

My husband knows more—he does not always understand, and that's okay—but knows how to help me, pray for me, and give me space. It has been beautiful to experience the love of Jesus through Eric—to see Jesus with skin on (he hates when I say that), but he is truly embodying Jesus and being his hands and feet. I have been able to understand what others are going through and ask the hard questions.

The medication and community began to do good work in my life, and I became incredibly grateful that I had stayed clinging to the Word. I knew I was safe with Jesus. With growing confidence in the truth and hope in the Word as the fog lifted, I was aware of negative spirals and lies and learned to stop them. It was not seamless or quick. I had lots of bad days. And slowly, those days got further and further apart. Now, when I recognize the signs from my brain and body, I have ways to function.

It's not just about coping. It's about living.

My mountains haven't gone away. They are still there, alongside me as I continue on this journey. Sometimes, they get in the way, but I'm okay with it. I now know how to cry out to God and that it's okay to cry. I know how to grieve with those who grieve and rejoice with those who rejoice. I know that I am not alone. I want you to know you are not alone.

In the pit of depression, I borrowed prayers from the book of Psalms as a means to communicate with my Creator. I had no words for all the feelings. The authors of the Psalms wrote songs to express praise, pain, anger, and many other emotions. I used the Psalms as my groans for help when I did not know how to communicate with God. I have merged some of those into a prayer. It is not perfect; it is a simple plea for anyone who must stay in place but may not be in a safe space—emotionally, physically, or mentally.

I pray this over you as you read this book:

Lord, have mercy on me. Do not be deaf to my call to you. Hear my silent cries and heavy weeping in this dark place.

I feel like all have forsaken me, but I know you will bring me in.

Only you can hold me close right now.

I have tried to be happy, and I have tried to be strong. But my soul is full of sorrow. I wait for you.

I know you are near; my soul quickens when I read your Word. I see the peace.

Lord, my God, be my joy and be my strength. Only you can bring me peace when I lay down and sleep and rise.

You, O Lord make me dwell in safety. Even though I know your safety can look different, I know you are good.

As I suffer according to your will, may I entrust my soul to you, my faithful Creator.

Amen.

things to think about

I hope and pray God shows up for you
and you can notice how he is moving.

1. Are you willing to reach out for help?

2. Will you connect and be honest with God, to hash it out with him?

3. Are you willing to continue with the pain as the journey continues toward healing?

4. Do you recognize your mountains or deserts?

seven

fear of failing

Have you ever found yourself stuck in the middle? This is where I found myself, as I was trying to do good, attempting to stop people-pleasing and healing from deep depression. I did not want to go back to where I had been and who I was, and at the same time, I was terrified to go forward.

I had to move forward in this journey out of the wilderness. I thought I had put enough work into improving myself to move into the promised land. Some aspects of myself were stuck in the wilderness, needing to be worked out and peeled away, like fear and not feeling like I was enough. It has always been frustrating to me that not all of me can move forward with a steady, together pace of growth. I know and believe that is a work of grace. I am not sure I could have handled doing all the inner work or the growth at the same time. Two steps forward and one step back it is.

We are going to jump straight into the story of the Israelites to see what they are up to in their journey. We've ended the book of Exodus, and now we are taking a hop, skip, and jump over to Leviticus. You're welcome. This book contains all of the instructions for how the Israelites were to live, set apart and holy. Let's just say that I am rather happy to live on the New Testament and Jesus side of time because we don't have to do all the sacrifices and such. However, I wouldn't mind keeping the rule that women have to leave the camp during their menstrual cycle (Leviticus 15:16-24). A week off each month would be nice. So, we'll move right along into Numbers, the book after Leviticus, which continues their wilderness journey.

The Israelites packed up the Tabernacle and headed north from Mount Sinai with the covenant renewed and a fresh hope in God's plan and presence. They, too, were approaching a situation where they were starting to feel good—confident in the Lord's presence and having some clear instructions. They kept up their complaints about the food and water situation but continued to move forward. God instructed them to head to the promised land and enter! He also reminded them, "Do not be afraid! Do not be discouraged!"

Cue the foreshadowing music...

They got to the border, jazzed up but a little nervous. The leaders sent a team of scouts in first, a man from each tribe, including, Joshua, Moses' assistant. They were to go in and report what the land, food, and people were like. The twelve spies were gone for 40 days. The Israelites waited without rebellion, complaining, or idol-building all 40 days.

When the twelve returned, they had a beautiful bounty (perhaps some grapes and pomegranates) and reported of a wonderful fertile land. Would we expect anything less from a land God said would be flowing with milk and honey? Then, ten of the scouts sent a ripple of fear over them. They declared the people in the land were mighty! Some were descendants of giants, they said, like from the stories we heard from our grandparents. The ten men worried and shook up the crowd saying, "We are not able to go up against the people, for they are too strong for us" (Numbers 13:31).

The other two men, Joshua and Caleb, combated this negative talk. They reminded the people that God was with them! Remember, do not be afraid or discouraged! They should enter now and take what he had given and promised them!

But the people cried and complained against Moses and Aaron that whole night. They wanted to go back to Egypt. The Israelites chose not to remember all that God had done for them. They even threatened to stone Moses and Aaron, but God showed his glory to the people and asked, "How long will you not believe and trust me?" (Numbers 14:1) God was righteously frustrated. Moses interceded (again) and asked God to continue showing his glory to the world by keeping the Israelites alive and not wiping them from the planet. God agreed, but as punishment for their mistrust in his plan, none of the doubters were allowed to enter the land. They would wander 40 years, one year for each day they scouted. The next generation would enter the promised land. All those who saw the miracles of leaving Egypt would die in the wilderness, except for Joshua and Caleb. These two would get to enter the promised land in 40 years for they believed in God and were faithful to trust him.

Moses shared all this with the people, so they would understand what their rebellion would cost them. They were not to enter. Only their children would get to see and inhabit the promised land.

Y'all, the next morning, they were like, "Okay, we slept on it and talked about what God said, so now we are ready to go! Let's take that land." *Facepalm.* They wanted to be all on board after hearing the consequences of disobedience. How often are we like that?

Poor Moses. He's like, way to rebel again! He reminded them that this was not what God had in mind. If they entered the promised land now, God would not be with them, and the Israelites would enter without protection. Moses told them they would fall by the sword. They entered into the promised land ready for battle anyway...it did not go well.

Joshua and Caleb wanted the Israelites to enter the promised land after they returned from the spy mission. They dared to go without worrying about the strength of those they would be fighting. They trusted God to do what he said he would do. No fear; God was with them. They could see their future flourishing. They resolved to be steadfast in their faithfulness and belief in God's promise. These two qualities gave me hope for being able to walk into my own wilderness. Caleb and Joshua may have been afraid of what their friends thought of them, but they dared to show the Israelites the hope and goodness God had promised them. Even in what they knew would be hard.

Fear can point us in the wrong direction or keep us stuck. I was so afraid of not doing enough good to please God (this is a lie we will address in the next chapter). I was so full of fear that I would swing back and forth on a pendulum from being good to doing good. I wanted to continue the journey of shedding my people-pleaserness but was also afraid of the things I would have to give up.

I could relate to the story in Numbers of the Israelites being stuck in the middle, knowing what to do, wanting to walk in obedience but afraid to do it. As I came out of the darkness of depression, I saw hope of functioning in life, but I felt stuck. I was trying to be neutral, to not care what people thought of me and to convince myself that God thought well of me, all while trying to do good.

In his book, *Culture Making*, Andy Crouch writes about creating new things. The Israelites were supposed to be going into the promised land to create a new culture set apart from the rest of the world. But they continued to be surer of themselves, both with fear and pride, than of God's plan for them despite seeing how God had shown provision, security, and his glory. Andy says, "We will end our efforts to change the world exhausted and spent, less sure of ourselves and less sure of God—

or, worse we will end surer of ourselves and less sure of God."[1]

I wanted to create something new in my life, but because I was saying yes to all the good, I was exhausted and less sure of what God had for me. I had people telling me that I was thinking too much about a calling and purpose and trying to find it in everything I did. I am creative, so I think I needed to find the passion and worth in everything that I'm doing. *I know.* That is a huge amount of pressure. I didn't know at the time how to shift that intensity, and to be honest, I still have trouble with it. As I learned to pay attention to where God was moving and name the things that were not for me, I found overwhelming peace—the only kind God can give.

At the time, I saw I was entering the wilderness, not the promised land, I was giving up the idea of who I thought I should be according to the people around me. I was learning to let go of worrying about my future, what others thought, and embrace the unknown. My wilderness was going to be for learning, grieving and developing courage. I needed to resolve to keep going in the direction God was leading and know I would not be alone in the journey.

The source of my fear, of not being good enough and being too much, was the unknown. I had the need to create purpose for everything I did. Rest made me feel like I was not enough of the human God made me to be. That I could not live up to his ultimate purpose for me. I felt like I was too much to those around me as I tried to find a meaning for all of the things

I committed to. I thought I was exhausting to listen to, so I had a hard time voicing my convictions or opinions.

What if instead, we choose not to care about others' opinions. We choose to put our effort into creating and cultivating what God is moving us to do. I want to care about that. It was time to turn from the fear at least for the moment. I felt like I needed a daily physical reminder of this decision to move forward. In the Bible, the Israelites used stones called an Ebenezer to lament, ask for help, give a sacrifice, or show victory. Making a stack of stones didn't have the permanence I felt I needed, but I did have my body. So, I got a tattoo.

I got a tattoo in solidarity with a friend. I was marking victory—my brain was feeling better. I was marking the lament of being good and a people-pleaser. I was asking God to be my help. I did not and could not do this alone.

> To this end also we pray for you always, that our God will count you worthy of your calling, and fulfill every desire for goodness and the work of faith with power, so that the name of our Lord Jesus will be glorified in you, and you in him, according to the grace of our God and the Lord Jesus Christ. (2 Thessalonians 1:11-12)

The tattoo is on my right wrist and says, "Resolve to do good." I wanted it visible for me and the conversations that would come up because of it. I needed a mark to help me be bold when

I was saying no and help me focus on what God hoped for me. This would all happen in my wilderness journey over the next few years. Resolving to do good.

I pray you find your Joshua and Caleb. The people and the spiritual practices who will help you find the courage to continue the journey when discouragement and fear are pushing you to turn back to your old ways.

things to think about

*I hope and pray God shows up for you
and you can notice how he is moving.*

1. Do you feel like too much or not enough to others?

2. Can you create your own Ebenezer to mark your movement forward?

3. What symbol would be meaningful to you?

eight

how Jesus related to the triune God

I began to dislike that each time I felt like I stepped forward in becoming who I thought God wanted me to be there was something else to work on. I'd take two steps backward, or pain would stick around. No matter how many times I asked God to take away my depression, anxiety, and some of the other struggles mentioned, he would say, No or Not yet.

Sometimes, my thoughts would spiral with doubting questions: *Why couldn't he? Why didn't he? Is he really good?* Then I would wonder about all the other horrible things in the world that are so much bigger than my pain. Why would he even care about little old me? I am just out here living in suburbia. I cannot do huge things to change the world. I want to, but I don't think I can.

Jesus makes all things new including our relationship with ourselves—including our thoughts. Over the last few chapters, I have exposed some of my struggles (pride, anxiety, depression, to name a few) and how I brought them to God. I did not always want to do this introspective work, but Jesus has shown me how to be kind to myself. I hope that you have been able to sit and be honest with yourself and God. You might have found some darkness or pain—hurt from a relationship, physical pain, spiritual abuse, or many other things.

Our friend Jesus beckons us to look at his life, learn from him, and ask different questions. How can it be that being quiet is also a warrior pose? How can that be? That being at Jesus' feet is better than serving the many? How can it be? That loving the one, not looking for anything in return, and getting on with your day is enough? That I am enough without doing a lot? How can it be?

Jesus showed us how to relate to and be kind to ourselves. This chapter was difficult to write because I tend to be hard on myself, something Jesus does not do to himself, his disciples, or me. Because of his grace and mercy, he has led me as I prioritized working on my inner self.

In the New Testament, Jesus gave us the new laws of love for those who would choose to believe in him and live a set-apart holy life. He knew we could follow in his steps because he left the Holy Spirit to dwell in each of us when he ascended to heaven.

Moses received the laws in Exodus expanding them in Leviticus and then gave those instructions to the Israelites.

Jesus sat on a mountain with the disciples next to him, the crowd in front of him, and brought new life into those Jewish laws. Jesus expanded and flipped the laws on their heads in Matthew 5-7. He began with the beatitudes and delivered these new commands for a holistic upside-down kingdom. As he taught, he drew on what the people knew. "You have been told..." was repeated over and over as he went through the laws given by God through Moses on Mount Sinai.

And for me? It gave me hope in the three areas where I could see the lies I believed (identity, idolatry, and rest) and helped me to work through them with the truth.

Identity

> "Let your light shine before men in such a way
> that they may see your good works and glorify
> your Father who is in heaven." (Matthew 5:16)

Meditating on this verse helped free my mind from things I thought I should be doing or thought I had to do. Instead, I would ask, "What good does God have for me to do today?" I can do all things, but I am not made for everything. God has named me and called me to do certain things (Exodus 31:1-11). It was time to begin to whittle down what those were. I did a lot of journaling and reflecting on things that brought me joy and things that brought me anxiety.

In Exodus 31, God told Moses that he had given the gifts to others for creating all the things for the Tabernacle. Similarly, he has created each of us to do good works. Jesus reminds us that in whatever we do, we can be a light (a physical presence of God's love and hope) that draws people to God and glorifies him. Figuring out how to remind ourselves of this identity—a light in the darkness—will be something we search for together. The key to this identity feature of God is that it doesn't matter what you are doing—student, barista, IT, doctor, teacher—we can take our talents and gifts and use them to show God's love and hope to all we interact with.

Idolatry

> "No one can serve two masters; for either he will hate the one and love the other, or he will be devoted to one and despise the other. You cannot serve God and wealth." (Matthew 6:24)

> "But let your statement be, 'Yes, yes' or 'No, no'; anything beyond these is of evil." (Matthew 5:37)

The first commandment is to love God and not have other things take priority over him (Exodus 20:1-7; 24:9-11). My law abiding, morally right, especially if it looks good—also known as legalism—past looked like me saying yes to someone but promising above and beyond and thus breaking my boundaries, and seeking to please people. As I began to meditate on the verses above, the Holy Spirit revealed that I had not been putting God first. I journaled the question: "Am I building my kingdom or God's

Kingdom today?" This question had the potential to become legalistic, but it was a start for me to recognize whether I was living in joy and building with God or striving to please myself and those around me.

My other master is not always money; I think it truly depends on the situation. Sometimes it's friends, my kids, the news, etc. Whichever thing truly has a grip on my attention. We cannot serve two masters. Once again, it is easy to say but not to do. It becomes a choice each morning. What are we building here on Earth? Are we co-creating with the thought of the future heaven, or are we building a little kingdom for our needs and wants? Are we meeting the needs of those around us while creating what God has for us, or are we holding onto what we are making?

Rest

> "So do not worry about tomorrow; for tomorrow will care for itself. Each day has enough trouble of its own." (Matthew 6:34)

Matthew 6:25-34 ties into the above just as well, but if we take a moment to focus on verse 34, we can see a form of rest. This rest, just focusing on today's worries and not tomorrow's, allowed my brain to be still and be present. Jesus gives us permission to not worry about tomorrow. The act of being present has been a gift to me. I learned to find rest in quiet moments when I was not enveloped in all the worries and anxieties of things to come.

I was able to sit in silence. Meditating on these verses allowed me to have hope for my future while living in the day.

I frequently thank the Father that he sent his son, Jesus. He paved the way to loosen me from the Old Testament laws that I twisted into legalistic chains. I'd much rather live a wild adventure with Jesus building his kingdom come.

How does Jesus show us how to deal with inner struggles?

In chapter 6, we talked about our struggles in the darkness and how we long for God to walk with us, so we know we are not alone and are on the path towards light and healing. We looked at questions like: Where is God in this? Where am I with God? Let's explore how Jesus cares for us in this darkness.

Jesus shows us how to be kind to ourselves in our becoming. He loved himself. He knew everything he did was for the glory of God (the Trinity—Father, Son, Holy Spirit) and reflected that glory in love. John 1:14 says, "And the word became flesh and dwelt among us, we have seen his glory, as of the only Son from the Father, full of grace and truth."

Later in John, there is an evening when Jesus was probably hanging out with the disciples in the house they were Airbnb-ing in Jerusalem. There was a quiet knock on the door. It was Nicodemus, a member of the Jewish council. The whole place was quiet as Nic asked if he could speak with Jesus. Jesus said yes. He didn't say, "Let's talk about this tomorrow," or "Man, if your colleagues knew you were having these thoughts, you would be tossed out of your job." Maybe Jesus took him into the next room so he would be comfortable or they went outside for some fresher air. Nic asked his questions, and Jesus answered.

When Jesus said a very well-quoted verse in John 3:16 (for God so loved the world...), he was speaking in the still of the night to Nicodemus. There was much more to this conversation, but I would like to point out how Jesus cared for Nic.

We get to see Nic's faith grow, because later in John 7:50-51, Nic stands for his convictions by risking his place in the Sanhedrin to protect Jesus. To love others as ourselves, we first have to know who we are and love ourselves. If we do not love ourselves, can we be honest with ourselves? If we cannot love ourselves, can we truly love others? This is a big challenge because, of course, you love your people! But when we accept our brokenness and believe who God says we are, then I would argue we can look at the rest of humanity a bit differently. It all ties back to identity.

When we are in the pit of things, it is hard to see the possibility of getting out of the darkness. Going to Jesus may not fix everything, but he will be near to answer our questions and guide us.

How does Jesus show us how to cast out fear of others' opinions and walk in obedience?

In the first few verses of Matthew 14, John the Baptist, Jesus' cousin, was beheaded by the current ruler (vv. 1-11). Jesus learned about it during a day of ministry. He went to the water, got in a boat, and was alone (v. 13). I wonder what it was like for Jesus, the God-man, to experience grief as a human. As he spent time in nature, talking with his Father, he eventually arrived back on shore and the sick were waiting. Jesus saw the people and had compassion for them (v. 14). Over the course of the day, he taught and multiplied bread and fish to feed well over 5,000 people (vv. 15-21). When ministry was done, he sent his disciples away, said goodbye to the crowd, and headed up the mountain to be alone (vv. 22-23).

What a huge range of emotions and physicalness Jesus had to stay present for. He knew he had to get away! Into solitude to recharge and talk with his Father. This alone time was fellowship with the Godhead. Jesus filled up so he could pour out. If *he* needed this time to be with the Father, how much more do we need it?!

In verses 24-33, Jesus walked on the water to catch up with the disciples. It was late in the night, and the boat was being battered by the waves. As Jesus approached, they thought he was a ghost and freaked out.

> He says, "Take courage! It is I; do not be afraid!" Peter said to him, "Lord, if it is you, command me to come to you on the water." And he said, "Come!" And Peter got out of the boat, walked on the water, and came toward Jesus. But seeing the wind, he became frightened, and beginning to sink, he cried out, "Lord, save me!" Immediately, Jesus stretched out his hand and took hold of him, saying to him, "You of little faith, why did you doubt?" When they got into the boat, the wind stopped. (Matthew 14:27-32)

Jesus encouraged Peter in the moment to be strong and courageous, to believe, focus on him, and to walk the straight path...on a freaking lake in the middle of the night! Peter jumped ship and walked but had a flash of reality that he was a human walking on water and panicked (maybe looking to the left and right, taking his eyes off Jesus). Jesus was right there just like he promised. He grabbed him immediately. I don't see Jesus' question to Peter as a shame or a scolding question. I see him pulling him close and being like, *Why did you worry about anything else? When your focus is on me you can be like me. You can do what I can do and even greater things* (John 14:12). Grace.

When we work with God and push most of these things (fear, idolatry, pride) out by being mindful, even while walking through grief, we meditate on the Word to know and believe who we are and that we are loved.

So, how do we do all these things? I know we do them with the Holy Spirit, but Jesus also intercedes for us. Moses spoke with God when the Israelites did not know what they wanted or needed. Jesus does that for us, too!

In Deuteronomy 2:7, Moses told the Israelites, "For the Lord your God has blessed you in all the work of your hands. He knows you're going through this great wilderness. These forty years the Lord your God has been with you. You have lacked nothing."

We may not see it yet since we are only halfway through the Israelites journey, but God had always provided everything they needed to make it through. I believe you and I will lack nothing with Jesus interceding for us. It just might look different than what we expected. Oh, how he loves us! How Jesus understands us because of his fully being human and fully being God.

Jesus had to intercede on my behalf, as I still didn't fully trust him. I didn't even last 40 days. There were so many days when I was struggling with fear, depression, or living for others that I did not even go to him, read the Word, or pray. I saw him continuing to intercede for me. He worked around me and through my friends, and I would see glimpses of his glory that would guide me gently back to him. I know so many people see a big vengeful God of the Old Testament and a meek Savior in the New Testament. But to truly see that they are the same God—yesterday, today, and tomorrow—is a gift we can have. Seeing the God of Moses as the same God that came himself down to Earth to live with us reveals the beautiful picture of a God who wants a relationship with us. With each new interaction, he wants to move closer and closer to being in real relationship with us, indwelling within us through the Holy Spirit.

We will continue to struggle with hard questions: Where is God in this? Where am I with God? Where did Jesus show us where God was and where he was with God? While we may not always understand what is going on and may sometimes feel out of control, we can look to our God who has made everything, yes everything, beautiful throughout time and in its own time.

I pray this over you, my friends. That you know you are worthy of what God has called you to. In rest, work, and fun. May you resolve to do good in everything through faith and his power. May God be glorified as you point to him. May others see your joy and long for the grace of God in their lives. (*Inspired by 2 Thessalonians 1:11-12*)

things to think about

*I hope and pray God shows up for you
and you can notice how he is moving.*

1. Can you be honest with yourself?

2. God can handle and wants to hear all of your
   emotions; can you be honest with him?

Part Three

Doing Good; Still Exhausted and
Relating to the World

nine

the self-righteous complainer

As you move from being good to doing good, there will be competition within your soul. Fighting over old ways and new ways—wisdom from above or earthly wisdom. You will have to decide which one you will listen to. We are now moving onto something even bolder; we are going to choose to do the good works set before us for God's glory. Each time we have moved forward, step by step, we are making more of our choices with God, which brings freedom and glory to his name.

I have found three things still put up a fight when letting go of this people-pleasing business. I want to prove myself to those around me, but I try to cover it up and it comes out in these ways—exaggerating, complaining, and competition. For me, these stem from busyness, exhaustion, expectations, and (you guessed it) pride.

Exaggerating

We'll do this one first. I hate that I exaggerate. Why do I do it? I want you to think my story is funnier, I am smarter, or I am cooler. (Gosh, I am in my late 30s and still want to feel cool; sorry kids, it does not go away!) This comes out in my physical actions or verbally. Am I animating myself to feel larger than life? Am I using my words to produce a false truth?

Complaining

I become a complainer when I am busy especially when I say yes to something I know I should have said no to. When I complain, it gives me a crappy attitude. Is my ego hurt? Was someone just doing their job? Am I only looking at myself in the situation? Is the complaining tied to an exaggerated story?

Competition

We have sayings like, "It's good to have some friendly competition." But is it? Is it good to be competing? Even in a friendly board game, it brings out an ugly side. I will win or else! At all costs, my pride will not be damaged! That may be a bit extreme, but to some, those are the stakes. Unfortunately, I have allowed myself to act that way and take friendly competition and make it fierce. It comes out in raising kids, or getting the lead for a project, or having the most likes and comments on a social media post. What does that turn us into? We are full of jealousy and self-ambition. Now, if you can do all of this without feeling competitive, let me know how you are doing it.

These characteristics, exaggeration, complaining, and competition tend to show up in the Israelites' journey when they are exhausted or their expectations are not met. They arrived in the Desert of Zin, and Miriam, Moses and Aaron's sister, died. God told the Israelites the older generation would die and their children would enter the promised land and flourish there. Throughout the rest of Numbers and Deuteronomy (their timelines weave together), we see the old generation gradually pass away through old age, rebellion, and war.

After Miriam died, the Israelites complained. There was no water! They complained and wanted their old life back. Again. They would have rather died as slaves in Egypt with water and food. They questioned Moses again.

Complaining and comparing. How quickly they forgot. How quickly we forget. Moses and Aaron did not know what to do. They went to God and fell onto their faces. God gave very specific instructions.

1. Take Aaron's walking stick.

2. Speak to the rock.

That's it. Moses followed the first step, and then he abandoned the plan. "Listen now you rebels; shall we bring you water for you out of this rock?" (Numbers 20:10, emphasis mine). He was angry and frustrated. He hit the rock twice instead of speaking to it.

Did you catch that when Moses spoke? He said "we," referring to himself and Aaron, not God. Moses had now done the same thing the Israelites had done. He forgot. He had just been in the presence of God, and he let his frustration out as he spoke and hit the rock twice to bring water forth.

God told Moses and Aaron that neither would enter the promised land. He said they did not trust him; they did not represent God as holy to Israel when they failed to follow the steps to bring water out of the rock. God's holiness and glory are always primary. He does not mess around with it.

So, Moses hit the rock instead of speaking to it. What's the big deal? They did not represent God as holy to Israel. They did not believe God. He told them they wouldn't be leading the next generation into the promised land.

At the end of the chapter, they reached Mount Hor. God asked Moses, Aaron, and Aaron's son, Eleazar, to climb the mountain. It was time to pass the priesthood to the next generation. The priesthood was a role of spiritual authority over Israel. The high priest's role was hereditary in Aaron's family, and it would pass from generation to generation (Exodus 29:9). Eleazar would be leading the next generation of Israelites into the promised land. Moses gave Eleazar the garments of the priesthood, and Aaron died on the mountain. The community mourned for 30 days (Numbers 20).

Let's pause for a second and maybe take a couple of breaths.

To be honest, I don't totally get it, and this chapter in the Bible makes me sad and a little angry. I tear up knowing the whole story. Moses, Aaron and Miriam (Micah 6:4) led this crazy generation for decades. Moses watched his siblings, Aaron and Miriam, die. Then he got the news he wouldn't go into the promised land after all this time. I know God keeps those who lead to higher standards, but I don't fully understand. So, I'm choosing to trust God, and the story, and keep going.

We know that parts of us will die while we are wandering the wilderness. The point is to grow. For that to happen, death occurs to make room for that growth. In the wilderness journey of doing good, I noticed myself depending on my own strength. I was not trying to please people anymore, but I attempted to do many things by myself. This time was meant for growth and shedding old habits, but I created new unhealthy ones.

Following my standards, not God's, led me to complain, compete, and exaggerate. Doing good took top priority. This self-righteousness had become a new law of doing good. While that sounds better than people-pleasing, it wasn't. I made this weird rule of resolving to do something good in my community, home, church, and work every day of the week. If I didn't hit my goals, I gave myself no grace. I was distracted and striving to be the greatest. I just didn't know it yet.

Because of this, I had become a complainer. I noticed it most when I struggled to finish all the good things I said yes to. When I became overwhelmed, I would complain about the same thing I knew I should have said no to.

I had begun competing with myself. How much good was I getting done, and was it enough? I became impatient and easily frustrated when my perfect timing didn't come to fruition. I was examining my life. I would start comparing myself to others—their success, their looks, their life.

As the Israelites wandered the wilderness, God provided all the reminders for how to do good and be set apart. They had laws, feasts, and sacrifices. God gave them the best he could without Jesus.

While sitting with God, I would read, journal, and listen. I know this is not ideal for everyone, but it is how I was able to help focus my racing and do all the good thoughts. I might ask, *Why am I feeling this way? What are they doing better that I'm seeking to beat them at? Do I need to walk away from the situation or walk towards it?*

I was learning to hold everything with open hands. And I was learning to name things. I have found that my named reasons usually lead to the deeper issue of pride. I turned my awareness of complaining and comparing into a time to communicate with God. I began using my complaining as an indicator of how overwhelmed I felt. I asked questions, like, *Why am I complaining about this?* or I assessed, *Is there something I can do about the situation? Do I take action by quitting, stopping complaining, or stopping and fixing the issue?*

I was hopeful to end the situation well and then had to resolve not to think about it anymore. I had a few Bible verses I would also memorize. I would reflect on them if the situation came to mind and brought me some anxiety. I found that if

I thought on good and lovely things, that's what would flow out of my heart and, hopefully, my mouth.

> Finally, brothers and sisters, whatever is true, whatever is honorable, whatever is just, whatever is pure, whatever is lovely, whatever is of good repute, if there is any excellence and if anything worthy of praise, dwell on these things. The things you have learned and received and heard and seen in me—practice these things, and the God of peace will be with you. (Philippians 4:8-9)

Sometimes, I am already in the know and just complaining to complain. It might be because someone I am around a lot has a habit of doing it, so I pick on something and complain. When it is evident this is happening, I tell someone to keep me accountable. Having someone who will help my conversations stay in the arena of good and lovely things gives me the courage to stop complaining.

If I decided to walk towards the problem, I figured out how to be gentle and encouraging to that person or situation. I ask God to give me words of wisdom to calm my racing mind and to keep me from being sassy in the conversation.

When I saw myself comparing, I have to get honest with myself. First, I ask why I am feeling this way? What are they doing better at that I seek to beat them? Second, do I need to walk away from the situation or walk towards it? Third, if I walk away, how do I fill my head with lovely things? If I walk towards it, I figure out how to be gentle and encouraging to that person or situation. I ask God to give me words of wisdom and support and to calm my racing mind from thinking it should have been me or why isn't it me?

Yes, we can try and do everything, but we know we can't. When we begin to release things, we have to lower our expectations, not because things won't be done right, but because other people could do it better, and it just might look different. What is holding you back? It might be you. What we do is a result of the heart. Are you prideful? Can you recognize when you need to step away? It's why we strive and wear ourselves out.

Proper expectations of myself, thinking of myself rightly, or trusting God with others and myself are ways I bring humility into the picture. Being a pushover at work, not setting boundaries, or giving up time with God to "serve" everyone else is not part of the humble picture.

You can say, "I quit" to your internal people-pleasing brain. I said I quit to allowing my appearance and perfect record to run my life and take control. Take Jesus. You know he is "God with us." Remind yourself daily, ask him to remind you—that's what the Holy Spirit is there for! Grab Bible verses that help you focus on your task—not on the person you are trying to be good for. Grab verses that bring rest and peace. Read them when you are done with work. Have boundaries. Tell your boss and co-workers those boundaries. You were great at sticking to a schedule; now stick to this one and be free.

James 3:13-18 is a set of verses I go back to again and again. Let me summarize the them. Wisdom from above is pure and produces good conduct and understanding. When we have jealous and selfish motives, everything becomes chaotic. What we do is important, but so is what we say. Good fruit brings peace.

I have had to say goodbye to things I truly loved—jobs, certain friendships. I left because complaining became my idol. Ugh. I put the weird companionship and people agreeing with me above God and what he thought of the situation. Searching for people to validate my complaining feelings meant it was time to move on—by pushing forward or stepping away.

There have been times that I have had to walk away from something because of a change of heart in me, because of Jesus, or because I should not have said yes in the first place. These situations are harder for me to walk away from because I have committed to someone or something. It is hard to say no to people we love, and I often feel like I disappoint them. I have learned that God covers it. If it is from him, he will move in the time, space, and person to fill the void.

The point of us being a holy and set apart people is that we are to look different from the world. We need to consider what could help us look different. Maybe taking away busyness is a good start? It was for me, but it was hard. It also left time for me to complain. I then also found myself competing with others (in my head and online). I was hopeful that quitting would help me feel free! But it took some adjustment to understand what freedom actually meant. Soon, I found that it might not just be quitting completely, but rather, checking my motivations or seeing how I could make the situation best for everyone. All easier said than done. I was learning to approach everything with open hands. God, if I need to go somewhere else, move me; if I'm here to stay, hold me through a hard time.

The goal is peace. Peace in my thoughts, words, and actions all working together to bring God glory.

things to think about

I hope and pray God shows up for you
and you can notice how he is moving.

1. What do you need to release?

2. How do you make the distinction between the work
   God wants you to do and what you think he wants
   you to do?

ten

convictions before confidence

It is only as we are found, through humility, in Christ that we are freed from longings for praise, honor, and prestige, freed from longings for material well-being, and freed from longings for power and influence. Wealth, the praise of others, and influence are not wrong in themselves; it is merely that the human person is prone to seek satisfaction in God's creation and God's gifts rather than in God himself.[1] - Gordon T. Smith, Beginning Well

Now, we will venture to talk about the importance of our confidence. It does not matter whether you had an "exciting life" or a "boring life." It does not matter whether you have had an "easy" or a "hard" life. I want you to know you matter. Your story matters. Why does your story matter? Well, I believe we are all created for the goodness of God. We are all created in his image, so in short, if he made you like himself, that means you mean something. You know "if-this, then-that"? If you are a human in the world, then you matter.

My story is nothing big. Nothing dramatic happened to me or my family to make me want to share my story. A big God did touch all aspects of my life in a way that I believe no one else could have. While you may not see anything drastic or miraculous happening to me, I do. I know it's happening. I can feel it. Even though my life looks like it is moving mostly normally in the suburbs, I feel, hear, see, and read that God is doing something within me because of the stories others have shared, and the impact those stories have had on me. I need to share how God has showed up in my life, and the wonder has called me to share.

Because of those stories and wanting to share my own, I had to look at confidence in what God had done in my life from a different perspective. Changing my thought process, decreasing my pride, and having the courage to face depression and anxiety and use it to move through life have allowed me to step out in obedience and walk in the freedom to live my best life in Christ. Let me tell you, most of those acts are small like calling a friend, supporting a mission, or being a part of Dressember. There are small things this one little human can do that can make a big difference in the long haul just like God making small changes in my soul. I want to implore you to see that the small things you do currently in life are making and will make a difference. We don't usually get to see them right away. I am just now seeing the fruit of some of the small things I did years ago.

We don't always get to be the farmer who does and sees it all. Sometimes we are a worker who only plants the seed, or only waters, or only harvests. Individually, these are not big acts. They are small actions moving forward in obedience. If we don't do those things, we know something will die. If we do them, something will grow.

When we say that our story is not big enough or it's too much to share, it is like we are seeking our whole life to be something we are not. We need to know what is unique in our story to move forward, grow, and own the person we are. All the factors in my story have made me, me. I would like to change some things in my life, but for the most part, if I didn't have those things, I would not have grown into who I am now. And turns out, I think I'm a pretty cool hang. I'm tired of searching for who I think I should be to other people. Now is the time to look and see who I was, to connect the dots, and see who I am becoming. I want to move forward doing the good works God has set before me as the person he has made me to be, and I hope you are ready and willing to do the same.

So don't listen to those lies about your story, like not being cool, too quiet, too loud, not enough, or being too much. When you fall into those lies, you will start to live in them. Trust me, once you realize the negative effects of living out those lies, you will want to run away as fast as you can from them. You will also realize that those lies are terrifying and can debilitate you—which is exactly what Satan wants. You will never want to go back to them. Do not walk in that false identity. I say not to walk in that false identity and fall for the lies because I did. Do not be okay with that. Now that I look back at who I "was" over the past years, I feel great remorse that I allowed myself to grieve for what I believed were the perceived thoughts of others. I created this false identity out of what I thought other people thought of me. Y'all, that's crazy! Now that I am aware of that false identity, I can see it creep in during times of stress and intimidation. I don't want it to take over again. I know who I am in Christ and have a voice to speak truth. I do not have to stay silent for myself or others. I am learning to be an advocate for Jesus, myself, and others. He is an advocate for us. He has sent the Helper, the Holy Spirit, to guide us. So why not use it for the good of those around us when he moves us to do so?

I hope that something resonates with you on this journey. That you can reflect at the end on what God has done in your life and how he is forming you to do the good works set before you.

In the following passage we get to see a different perspective on how others viewed the Israelites during their journey in hopes that it will show us the confidence we can have. The characters in this story in Numbers feel wildly out of place. It has three characters: a donkey, Balaam, and Balak.

The story opens with Balak, a king set on cursing the Israelites, who saw the Israelites encroaching on his kingdom. He was worried and needed to figure out a way to defeat them for he knew his army could not. Balak knew of this guy, Balaam. Whenever Balaam called on a god to bless or curse a person/people, it usually happened in the asker's favor. So, he believed he could buy Balaam's correct divination against the Israelites.

Balaam was a seer of the gods—a.k.a., a non-Israelite that did not consult the one God, Yahweh, in divinations. The following is not me elevating him but sharing a 3,000 ft. view of the story and how we can apply the themes to our lives. Scholars have a lot to say on this dude, and it's not all great.

Over the course of Numbers 22, 23, and 24, Balaam had a few choices. On the first visit, Balak's men approached him with royal gifts and exuberant pleas to come with them. He could have seen the money and said, "Yup, I'm in, let's go." He could have said, "No thanks, all good." Or he could have said, "Let me consult the gods." Which is what he did. He invited Balak's men to spend the night, and he hoped for a vision or word from a god in the night. Balaam said God (Yahweh) was not allowing him to go with them and sent them away. On the second visit, they brought the prospect of positions of honor for Balaam. He asked them to stay the night. When Balaam asked God what to do that night, he said he could go, but only if he did what God said.

Balaam goes to Balak in Moab and Numbers 22:22 says that God was angry with him. We don't know why. In fact, it's another mystery, but we might assume that the Lord looked at Balaam's heart and knew his true motives. Perhaps, he was secretly hoping for some of that glory that Balak promised.

On Balaam's path, an angel stood in his way. His faithful donkey tried to avoid it and even spoke to Balaam. She complained that he should not be treating her poorly because she was avoiding the angel in front of them. The donkey assured Balaam that she had always been faithful, so there was no reason to be so rude. I love that Balaam didn't even bat an eye at her speaking to him but was more annoyed with how she was acting. When the angel was revealed to him, Balaam confessed his sin and said he would go back home. The angel instructed him to go on to Balak, and his army but only speak the words God gave him. (This is the interaction that led me to my assumption of him seeking some of his own glory alongside God's).

As he arrived, Balak came out and met him at the furthest border, annoyed that it took him so long. "So Balaam said to Balak, 'Behold, I have come now to you! Am I able to speak anything at all? The word that God puts in my mouth, that I shall speak'" (Numbers 22:38). What courage to say this to a king who had the money to pay you off or, by a snap of the finger, kill you!

Throughout Balaam's time with Balak, they built altars and made sacrifices to God, so they could hear what he wanted Balaam to say. Each time they got closer and closer to the Israelite's camp, finally being able to see them tribe by tribe, Balak's fear spiraled to frustration and then anger each time Balaam gave an oracle of blessing and not cursing! But Balaam was becoming more in awe of what God had done. He had heard the stories of what the Israelites had been through and knew God has blessed them and kept them. He kept his word and only said what God had given him.

It is a beautiful story of God's love and commitment to the Israelites. Even though Balaam may have come with the wrong motive, he saw what God had blessed. He would be a fool not to bless them as well.

In their final conversation, Balak's anger was kindled against Balaam, and he struck his hands together.

> Then Balak's anger burned against Balaam, and he struck his hands together; and Balak said to Balaam, "I called you to curse my enemies, but behold, you have persisted in blessing them these three times! Therefore, flee to your place now. I said I would honor you greatly, but behold, the Lord has held you back from honor." Balaam said to Balak, "Did I not tell your messengers whom you had sent to me, saying, 'Though Balak were to give me his house full of silver and gold, I could not do anything contrary to the command of the Lord, either good or bad, of my own accord. What the Lord speaks, that I will speak'? And now, behold, I am going to my people; come, and I will advise you what this people will do to your people in the days to come." (Numbers 24:10-14)

Balaam gave his final oracle. He prophesied of the destruction of those who opposed God.

What happened next? I thought this last verse of their interaction was so much louder than the talking donkey! "Then Balaam arose and departed and returned to his place, and Balak also went his way" (Numbers 24:25).

What in the world?! I mean, I know the Old Testament can be wild, but those were not the words I expected after a begging, angry, frustrated, possibly-ready-to-kill Balak lets Balaam go despite blessing Israel three times and prophesying destruction on Balak's people.

That last sentence sent me to read these chapters several times over. I was like, *What just happened?* How could I stand my ground in what I am convinced God has told me to do so much so that the people around me believe me and are confident in it? It also convicted me to look at my own motives when I do say yes? Am I looking for praise and honor of others (people-pleasing)?

What did it show me? I decided if I can have the confidence to say /do what God has given me to say/do, then it can change my motivation and convictions and bless others. Can I really believe what God has given me? Am I willing to say no to someone that has power over me? Am I willing to stand in the conviction of this confidence from my faith?

As I moved through answering these questions within the journey of doing good, I wished and hoped for the confidence to only speak what God had given to me and not compromise because of the honor of others or because of my lack of conviction.

The most visible way I was doing this was through work. Throughout this period, I had several jobs (part-time or free-lance because I was still mostly mom-ing). I would choose them because I thought it was part of my plan. But I kept finding that they did not fit where God was leading me. Why is this not fulfilling me? Why are these good things failing? I felt like Balaam on the donkey with my self-righteousness becoming the new law of doing good.

I was like Balaam on a mission to seek my purpose with confidence in myself, and God tossed situations in the way, helping, like the donkey, to keep me from the path of self-seeking. I mentioned a trip to Burundi, Africa earlier in the book. I continued to travel to Burundi because I began working for the organization. It was a path God guided me to, but it also felt self-seeking at times. God would redirect me to see life with a fresh perspective through the new classes of ladies coming through the program. The women leaned into learning about God and had so much excitement for the new life before them physically (because of the program) and spiritually (because of their new faith).

As the women progressed throughout the program, they learned about healing from their trauma, forgiveness, and God's love for everyone. They understood the power of education, learning skills, and Jesus. After finishing the program and graduating, the women would return on Fridays to share their testimonies of life before and now. Their convictions of knowing what is true, right, and possible of God are overwhelming. They know that people in the United States paid for them to get through classes and that their teachers helped them learn and grow. They know God is the one who orchestrated it all together for good and for his glory.

The reality of understanding justice in this place is that it allowed me to get into my emotions and the emotions of others and to not be afraid of them. If I did not take the time to learn and understand other people's stories, I couldn't be so open with my own. Not only that, but I would not understand how to come alongside others and bring shalom to this very broken world.

Why do I think convictions are needed in doing good for God's glory? There will be times to stand strong in your beliefs but also know which hills to let others stand on. I believe many things are not okay or should be changed, but I cannot take a stand on all of them. I must choose what I can be well-informed about, continue learning and asking questions, and decide what I believe to be true and why. I believe that if we are Christians, we might have convictions about what we believe. This allows us to know why we believe what we believe. It takes time, and there are many books and resources available. If you know what you believe and why, make a list of things that are non-negotiables for you as a Jesus follower.

Here are a few examples. Jesus came to earth to live a perfect life full of good works, miracles, and creating a community of believers. He healed, laughed, loved, ate, and cried. He showed us how to rest and how to act in righteous anger. His mission informed his convictions "to seek and save that which was lost" (Luke 19:10).

Moments before Jesus was to be arrested and led to the cross, he cried out to God, *Do I have to do this? Must I suffer?* He knew for you and me to walk with God, he had to endure the suffering and humiliation of the cross (John 17). He died on the cross, sinless, and perfect. When he died, he took on the weight of all the sins and put it on himself. He rose three days later. He showed his glorified body to his followers and many others before he ascended into heaven (John 19-20). He was no longer needed there physically because he was sending the Holy Spirit to live IN each one of those who believed in what he did (Acts 1).

These spiritual convictions bleed into my personal convictions. I think we should take care of the widows and orphans and displaced (all of them), and we should end human trafficking/slavery. I believe we should love our neighbors and speak to humans with dignity and love.

Each person has different convictions, and I think that is what keeps the world cared for and in check. While I will stand solid and do what I can to support my convictions, I must also listen to other perspectives and continue learning what they mean to me and the world. I have reconsidered things now that I once would not have agreed with because of new information or the Holy Spirit convicting me.

Where is my confidence? Is it in me? Is it in God? Do I think I've come to where I am because of my "goodness" and "righteousness"? Or is it because of God's goodness and righteousness? His mercy and grace are woven through my life.

When I lean on my own confidence, I feel like I fail. I have more anxiety and confusion about which path I should go on. I worry about past, present, and future. I worry I will make huge mistakes and never be able to recover. If I don't worry, I am overconfident. Overconfidence is good for no one. I don't want to have to think about what others—or even God—wants from me. I become cocky, sarcastic, and scattered. Balaam followed the directions of whatever god answered him, and when the true God answered him and he saw what God had done, Balaam changed his mind and did not curse Israel but blessed them.

When I put my confidence in God, things change, like my perspective, my attitude, and how quickly I do things. I become present. I am able to focus, not worrying what others are thinking about me; my hope is not of this world. I know life is fleeting, so why not lean on the creator of the universe? Then I can lean in with confidence in God, accepting criticism well, sleeping better, and approaching others with a bit more gentleness and patience. I desire to lean on him and please him. I want to shout for joy—I usually don't, but sometimes there is a happy dance.

I knew God was redirecting me, but I couldn't grasp what it was. It felt so different from what I had planned. Just like Balaam, each time he got closer to the Israelites, he saw how God blessed Israel. The same was happening for me. Each thing I quit moved me closer and closer to seeing what God had blessed; I could only be a fool and not accept it from him. What Balaam got to see and understand in days, took me much longer. None of this time spent searching for my confidence in him is a waste (as I believe nothing we do is wasted). The Holy Spirit has shown me I can learn from people and places in my life and that I need to grow in confidence and self-sufficiency.

In these chapters of Numbers, we saw God use someone outside his covenant to bless. If God can use Balaam and a donkey, there is a chance for us. May we continue to listen to his instruction and not go back to our old ways that lead to death.

things to think about

*I hope and pray God shows up for you
and you can notice how he is moving.*

1. Do you have a hard time making decisions?

2. Can you name why?

3. What do you do when you think you have made the "wrong" decision?

eleven

holding joy and sorrow

The very divine multiplication that gives us joy and delight in the
midst of our culture calling also leads us directly to the places
where the world is most in pain.[1] - Andy Crouch, Culture Making

Hold it loosely. I kept feeling God nudge me as we were ending
2017. It was a bit confusing. Hold what? My job? My volunteering? Church? My family? As I prayed, it became clear that he
was talking about my schedule and what I was committing
myself to do. I continued praying and journaling before the
new year hit. I felt a few things had to go, some things were
put on hold, and I vowed not to add anything unless it felt like
the best yes.

I planned to be intentional about listening to God's nudge
immediately and not delaying it. I was going into the new year

with open hands. I waited and listened to what I was supposed to respond to.

My grandpa died right before the new year rang in.

As soon as we got the call from my dad, I was ready to fly up to Oregon to see my grandma and help however I could. After communicating with everyone, we felt that, with my open schedule it was best I go when everyone was getting ready to leave. Then Grandma would not be left alone for a long stretch of time before the next family member would be with her. I went up a month later, overlapped with my parents, sister, and brother-in-law for a few days. Then they left, and it was just me and Grandma.

Those days were precious. Hard, but good. We sat together watching our favorite movies and shows. Grandma would tear up every now and then and share a story of Grandpa or their life of 67 years together, usually something funny. Or she would ask about the girls and Eric. We went shopping at the mall, looking for a new scarf. We navigated all the stores twice with her wheelchair so she could find just the right one. I left the nursing home after dinner. I went to my Airbnb to sleep and returned the next morning to hang out for the day. I stayed for a week and a half or so.

The night before I was going to come home I called Eric. I couldn't leave. I wanted to extend my stay. How could I just leave her all alone? The next day, I prolonged my goodbye as long as I could. I left with promises to bring my girls to see her as soon as I could. I tried not to cry leaving her apartment, but as soon as I sat in the front seat of my rental car, the grief overcame me.

It took all that was within me to drive that car to the airport and get on the plane. As the year continued, I tried to figure out how to hold some great moments of joy and more intense moments of grief.

Joy. An anniversary trip to Mexico. We felt like such grownups going to an all-inclusive resort we never thought we would be able to afford.

Grief. Deciding to move to a different church. We also did not leave well; we pretty much ghosted our friends, and I don't love that. At the time, we just did not know how else to do it.

Grief. My dad's side of the family gathered for my grandpa's internment service in Denver. I joined my mom and dad, leaving Eric and the girls behind.

Grief. Eric's grandpa died shortly after my trip to Colorado. We went to Oklahoma to help his mom and dad, with what we could with two littles.

Joy. I got to bring my girls to visit my grandma and fulfill my promise to her. We stayed with my aunt and uncle, and it was so nice to have that time with them.

Joy. I started teaching at a new university and got to travel there a few times to get ready for my classes.

Joy. A two-week trip to Burundi to document the amazing work going on at Homecare.

Grief ended the year. My grandma died right before Christmas.

Eric and I decided, on a whim, to bring the girls to Colorado after Christmas to see the snow. We were worn out and needed some nature and quiet. We rang in the new year snowed in and had the most magical time.

I was grateful for that time in the mountains to reflect on an oddly good year full of joy and grief. While I was grateful, I understood that getting snowed in could be rather stressful for some. I feel invigorated by travel, outside, and mountains. Pair that with time to reflect and enjoy my family. It was the chef's kiss.

As we make our way back to the story of the Israelites, we will fast forward to the end of Deuteronomy. In this book, Moses is reflecting on their story. He had four speeches to remind this group of what God had done. Why did he have to retell the story? Well, all the adults from the exodus of Egypt had passed away. Only their children were allowed to enter the promised land. Moses wanted to remind them where they had come from and all God had done. He instructed them on the law and covenant they had made with God and the blessings that would follow. He also reminded them of the curses promised if they did not.

I am sure there was a buzz in the crowd as they listened to Moses declare all of the things over a few days. They were camping near the Jordan River and preparing to cross to the promised land. They finally made it! I wonder if there was talk among them making sure they did not mess up like their parents and promising to do better.

Before his final speech, I'm sure everyone was excited! What was next? But then the Lord told Moses his days were coming to a close (Numbers 31:14); he would not be journeying on with them, and it was time to present Joshua as the next leader.

"So Moses went and spoke these words to all Israel. And he said to them, "I am a hundred and twenty years old today; I am no longer able to come and go, and the Lord has said to me, 'You shall not cross this Jordan.' It is the Lord your God who will cross ahead of you; he will destroy these nations before you, and you shall dispossess them. Joshua is the one who will cross ahead of you, just as the Lord has spoken. The Lord will do to them just as he did to Sihon and Og, the kings of the Amorites, and to their land when he destroyed them. The Lord will deliver them up before you, and you shall do to them according to all the commandments which I have commanded you. Be strong and courageous, do not be afraid or tremble at them, for the Lord your God is the one who goes with you. He will not fail you or forsake you."

"Then Moses called to Joshua and said to him in the sight of all Israel, "Be strong and courageous, for you shall go with this people into the land which the Lord has sworn to their fathers to give them, and you shall give it to them as an inheritance. The Lord is the one who goes ahead of you; he will be with you. He will not fail you or forsake you. Do not fear or be dismayed." (Deuteronomy 31:1-8)

The silence was probably deafening. Thoughts racing. *Moses came all this way! This is not fair! He is 120! How will we do this without him?! We just need to cross the Jordan!*

It was sad and wildly confusing that Moses did not get to enter the promised land with the rest of the Israelites. Deuteronomy 32:51-52 reminds us he did not trust God nor present God as holy to the Israelites at the waters of Meribah-kadesh. Like the scripture with Balaam, I don't understand.

I do think it was God's grace and mercy on him to have him not enter. In Deuteronomy 31:16-18, God tells Moses that the Israelites would begin entering the promised land well, but it would not last long. They would fall for the idols and break the covenant they just renewed. I don't know if Moses could make it through that heartbreak again watching the people he loved and led fall for the ways of the world instead of setting themselves apart as holy.

Deuteronomy ends with a song for them to sing to remember the commands and warnings of God and how to be a righteous people set apart. Moses ended his time with the Israelites with a final blessing over each tribe and passed the leadership on to Joshua. God offered Moses final instructions for his life. He was to go onto Mount Nero to see the promised land. God showed him all of it. I wonder if there was a super zoom so he could truly see it all. Then, God buried Moses. No one knows where he lay (Deuteronomy 34:6). The Israelites wept for him for 30 days.

Grief for the death of their leader, joy for making it to the promised land. As I journeyed through the wilderness to do good, paying attention to my people-pleasing tendencies, I shed the layers of lies that I told myself and the worries about what people thought of my choices. I learned to listen to what I was saying—was it time to leave or lean in? Through all that work and growth, I still had a hard time trusting God the first time. 2018 was the year that ingrained in me the importance and freedom of listening and doing what I heard him call me to. If I had not held my schedule and plans loosely, I don't know if I would have had that precious time with my grandma and been able to recount so clearly all the joy and grief that 2018 held.

I would begin to use breath prayers when I found myself in the midst of grief and uncertainty over those we are called to serve. As you inhale, address God. As you exhale, make a request of God. For example, I might inhale and say *Jesus*. I would exhale *have compassion on me.* May it help you and give you peace to do good works set before you to fulfill the glory of God alone.

This freedom of trusting God taught me the importance of sitting and listening. Life is more than just the good, and living comes with grieving. I cannot have joy and enjoy it until I know I am loved and pursued by my Creator.

In the day of prosperity be joyful, and in the day of adversity consider: God has made the one as well as the other, so that man may not find out anything that will be after him. (Ecclesiastes 7:14)

The greatest and worst thing of all of this is pain. You see, as we live for the glory of God alone, he will put us on the path of hope and joy, but also pain. Friends, this is okay. Do you see the tug and pull of joy and pain? This happens in our world. Because of grace and the cross, we get to keep moving forward with hope—even if it doesn't feel like there is any right now. There can be "abundance alongside suffering." We must go to God to seek comfort, confidence, and grace to move forward each day.

In my calling to my community, I get to be in great authentic relationships and enjoy their company. That authenticity leads us to share our happiness, pain, and sorrows. We will rejoice with those who rejoice and weep with those who weep. Living in this world or within our community is hard, and it is filled with joy.

My calling to use my creative work to help Hope4Burundi is full of joy and pain, too. I got to see that beautiful hope they exude after they learn about their true identity in Christ— adopted by the Lord Almighty. Before becoming healers of trauma, there is pain, sorrow, and worry. Their stories of how they got to where they are are difficult to listen to. But we push through the pain for hope and joy.

While writing this book, I have experienced hope, joy, and pain. I hope that going through these emotions and sharing them will let you see that we all experience this. Just because you have pain doesn't mean you can't have joy. Just because you have joy doesn't mean you won't have pain.

I used to live so afraid that I would look around each corner, waiting for God to spring some pain on me because I had joy. He's just not like that—at all. The grace and goodness that I accept from him and walk through life which leads me to broken places, in the best way possible. I trust him. I am wrapped in his grace so that I may help those in pain.

things to think about

I hope and pray God shows up for you
and you can notice how he is moving.

1. How do joy and grief look different in people's lives?

2. Is there a time when you held both?

twelve

how Jesus related to the world

...how much more will the blood of Christ, who through the eternal Spirit offered himself without blemish to God, cleanse your conscience from dead works to serve the living God? (Hebrews 9:14)

Overthinking, the swinging pedestal of exhaustion, and unsure how to handle my emotions brought me to see how Jesus handled the topics in these last three chapters. Jesus did not complain or compete, he was confident in what the Father had for him, and he knew how to hold joy and sorrow. He knew how to be deeply moved but not overwhelmed. A lesson I could use. Studying his life compared to the cycle that the Israelites went through at each new phase in their journey was eye-opening. I know Jesus is fully-God and fully-man, but seeing him be in very real human experiences *and* glorifying the Father, led me to wonder if I could bring glory to God while doing good, too.

Jesus had lots of things he could have complained or exaggerated about. I'm pretty sure he was the only one in his league as far as competition goes. Instead, he chose humble leadership. Let's look at a time in the Gospel of Luke when Jesus was hosted at Martha's home and had something to say about complaining and competition in the upside-down kingdom.

Luke 10 tells of a time when Martha was preparing her home to host Jesus, and she began complaining to Jesus that her sister Mary was not helping at all. In fact, Mary was sitting at his feet!

> But the Lord answered and said to her, "Martha, Martha, you are worried and bothered about so many things; but only one thing is necessary, for Mary has chosen the good part, which should not be taken away from her." (Luke 10:41-42)

I love the gentleness with which Jesus approaches Martha. He is not scolding her. He draws her near to see what is in front of her. Notice he did not say Martha was doing anything wrong, but that she was distracted from the best. Mary was able to perceive that sitting with Jesus, learning at the master's feet, was the best thing. I would like to note that in normal Jewish circles, when a teacher was teaching, women would not have been allowed; their place was in the preparation. So, for Jesus to say that she chose what was good, and that he welcomed it, would have been something astonishing for the women.

I am sure Martha went through many emotions, but perhaps she felt some relief knowing that her master was also releasing her from the competitive cultural standards of hospitality and she could choose to sit and learn from Jesus. And he welcomed her, too!

I used to be annoyed with this story, and I am not even sure why. As time went on, I began feeling convicted about not choosing the best thing. Out of stress, I complained, and usually, it was because of my choices. I had to be on social media a lot for work, and it was ruining what confidence I had as I began to compare everything I did. I had a time when I walked away from several conversations, realizing I had only complained or compared myself to others the whole time. As I was walking away, I had a gut feeling from the Holy Spirit saying, *Hey, let's work this out.* So, I did what Jesus said was best. I sat at his feet.

We will continue the journey of Jesus' friendship with Mary and Martha in John 11. Jesus was really good friends with their brother Lazarus, too. Lazarus got sick while Jesus was traveling doing ministry and healing people. Mary and Martha sent word to Jesus about what was happening, but he told his disciples they would wait a few days before going, for Lazarus' illness would bring glory to God. They were a bit confused, as usual. On their way to see Lazarus, Jesus revealed that he knew Lazarus was dead. It's a bit shocking when you don't know the story, but know that Jesus knows everything. How could he have waited until his friend died? Where was his urgency?

When they arrived, it was confirmed that he had been dead for four days. Martha was frustrated. She knew that if Jesus had been there he would not have died. Jesus then told her Lazarus would be raised to life. Mary came next. She fell at his feet weeping telling Jesus that he should have been there to save her brother. She said she knew he would be raised to life, but she thought Jesus was referring to his second coming (I do love that we have this from her; she has been sitting at his feet and learning!). She did not know that he meant to raise her brother right now! Jesus was deeply moved and troubled in his spirit. He hated seeing his friends in pain. He hated death, but it had to be a part of this life. I know we know God knows all, but as God-man, what does seeing that grief and sorrow look like? Does it feel like that pit in your stomach when there is nothing you can do but weep with those who weep?

And Jesus wept.

Do you picture silence? Everyone staring at the Messiah. Maybe they are confused because they know what he can do. Why didn't he save his friend?

Jesus went to Lazarus' tomb and asked people to roll away the stone. Martha reminded him that it had been four days, and the smell was going to be bad. He reminded her of their conversation just a little bit ago. That if she believed, she would see the glory of God—like right now!

Jesus sent a prayer to the Father, thanking him for hearing him and for always hearing him, especially for the benefit of the people around them. When he was done, he shouted, "Lazarus come out!" And Lazarus walked out, burial strips and all.

There are some things in this story that struck me in our year of grieving in 2018. Jesus did not reprimand any one for negative emotion around Lazarus' death. He had compassion on them. He felt what they felt. Between these two stories of Mary and Martha and Jesus, I love his true friendship with them. They felt comfortable to confront him with their worries and concerns. They were not afraid of a vengeful God. No, they knew that if they believed, they would see the glory of God—now or later—even if the situation didn't go the way they wanted it to.

This event was the turning point of Jesus' ministry. After Lazarus was raised from the dead, the religious leaders freaked out and plotted his death. Chapter 12 is jam-packed with the beginning of the end—everything from here on pointed to the cross and Jesus' confidence in God the Father. Jesus had been talking with Jews and Greeks. He identified himself as the Son of God, the light in the darkness. After some final words, he departed the crowd. John, the author of this book, indicated that even though Jesus had given them many signs, they still didn't believe. Many of the leaders believed him, but because of fear and being put out of their places of power, they would not confess. "For they loved the glory that comes from man more than the glory that comes from God" (John 12:42-43). How did he not feel defeated?

This truth hurts because sometimes I, too, choose the glory that comes from man over the glory that comes from God. I have seen mighty and small things in my life that can only be explained as works of God, yet I err in my old ways of loving the glory or people-pleasing. I lean on my confidence and self-sufficiency, but I fail. I have more anxiety and confusion about which path I should take. I worry about past, present, and future. I worry I will make huge mistakes and never be able to recover. If I don't worry, I am overconfident, and I become cocky, sarcastic, and scattered (like Balaam on his donkey).

So where is my confidence? Is it in me? Is it in God? Do I think I've come to where I am because of my "goodness" and "righteousness"? Or is it because of God's mercy and grace woven into my life?

> And Jesus cried out and said, "He who believes in me, does not believe in me but in him who sent me. And whoever sees me sees the one who sent me. I have come as light into the world, so that whoever believes in me will not remain in darkness...For I did not speak on my own initiative, but the Father himself who sent me has given me a commandment as to what to say and what to speak. And I know that his commandment is eternal life; therefore the things I speak, I speak just as the Father has told me." (John 12:44-50)

Jesus continued to say that he only spoke what the Father told him; he spoke with the Father's authority. He spoke with the confidence of God. He was not afraid of what people would think or do (in fact, he knew they were planning his path to the cross). He showed his confidence in God by going to the cross anyway. The Father asked his Son to be a light in the darkness by speaking truth, healing, and loving all who were lost. Jesus did all this for the glory of God.

Just as the Father gave him the words to speak, so does the Holy Spirit give us the words to speak when we ask him to. We receive that confidence when we believe Jesus. So what happens when I put my confidence in God? Things change.

My perspective and attitude change. I become present. I can focus and not worry about other's perceptions of me. I can accept criticism well. I sleep better. I have gentleness and patience. There are many indications that point to God's work because those are the hardest fruit of the spirit for me. They do not come naturally. My hope is not of this world.

I know I will eventually leave all this, so why not lean on the Creator of the universe and walk with confidence in what might seem a little crazy and impractical to the world? I desire to lean on him and please him. I want to shout for joy—I usually don't, but sometimes there is a happy dance, and I look a little weird.

I have seen the old and the new way of life in me, and I prefer the new. I fail to hold to it daily causing ups and downs in this life with Jesus. It is frustrating when you know how to walk in confidence but choose not to. I thank God again for the renewing of grace and hope each day.

At the end of Jesus' ministry, he experienced all of the human emotions—being betrayed by a friend, begging God to take the cross away from him, being accused of something he didn't do, being beaten, spit on, stripped, and then nailed to the cross.

Jesus took what was unbearable—all of the injustice and ugliness of the world—to the cross. He died for us so that we may, through the same power that raised him from the dead, walk through each day with enough grace to find joy in the midst of pain.

Jesus confidently knew his mission and purpose on earth. Throughout the Gospels, he takes time to check in with God by getting away and praying, sometimes all night.

Because of grace and the cross, we can bear suffering and keep moving forward with hope, even when (especially when) the grief is too heavy. That hope? It is the abundance that comes alongside suffering. We can go to God to seek comfort, confidence, and grace to move forward each day. Otherwise, when life is full of sorrow, it would be unbearable.

Jesus did just what he said he would do. He was raised from the dead and came out of the grave three days later. He first appeared to the women! He told them to go tell the disciples all that they had seen. He presented himself for 40 days around Jerusalem speaking to the people about the kingdom of God in his glorified body.

I love that Jesus ascended to the Father from the mountain as the disciples watched. Moses went to the mountain to see the promised land, and Jesus took his followers to the mountain to show them what the promised land in the new kingdom would look like. They were to go into all creation and proclaim the good news of all that Jesus had done. Just like Moses, Jesus did not get to continue with them on their journey. Moses left Joshua in charge of leading the Israelites. Jesus promised the coming of the Holy Spirit who would be their guide as the disciples went into the world!

things to think about

I hope and pray God shows up for you
and you can notice how he is moving.

1. What does it mean for your faith to know that Jesus experienced the same emotions that we do?

2. Can you name experiences that have brought you hope?

Part Four

Doing Good, Glorifying God,
and Living Fully Alive

thirteen

holy rituals

I find peace in some rituals, like lighting a candle when I write; it triggers my brain to calm down and focus. In October and November, I have Harry Potter on in the background as I clean the house and the air gets cooler. I journal most mornings to help me remember life and have a continuing conversation with God.

We left the Israelites getting ready to cross the Jordan River.

No longer confined to the wilderness, the Israelites enter into a freedom they had never known. Up to this point, they only had a hope of possible rest. Now, it was attainable in their lifetime!

It had been three days since Joshua 1, and it was time to move. God was still leading and, reminding them to follow the ark of the covenant because they did not know the way.

As the ark went ahead into the Jordan River, something amazing happened. The river dried up—just like God had said it would. Joshua 3:15 reminds us that the Jordan River banks overflowed during harvest, so it was no small feat to cross on dry land. Some of the Israelites were old enough to remember crossing the Red Sea with Pharaoh and his army chasing them 40 years before (Numbers 14:29-31). I can't imagine the excitement and some sadness for the loved ones who had died over the last 40 years and were not going in with them.

The priests were ordered to stand in the river while everyone passed on dry ground. When everyone had passed, Joshua commanded 12 men (one from each tribe) to go and gather a stone—like a big stone—from the riverbed. When the stones were gathered, everyone had passed through, and the priests and the ark moved to the other side, the Jordan River went back to normal. What a wonder that would have been.

What were the stones for?

> Those twelve stones which they had taken from the Jordan, Joshua set up at Gilgal. He said to the sons of Israel, "When your children ask their fathers in time to come, saying, 'What are these stones?' then you shall inform your children, saying, 'Israel crossed this Jordan on dry ground.' For the Lord your God dried up the waters of the Jordan before you until you had crossed, just as the Lord your God had done to the Red Sea, which he dried up before us until we had

crossed; that all the peoples of the earth may know that the hand of the Lord is mighty, so that you may fear the Lord your God forever." (Joshua 4:20-24)

The stones were for remembering. A way to tell their story to those who came after them. A way to see that God cared for them. It was a way to help me remember. God showed himself to the Israelites through so many miraculous and simple ways. We use these rituals to remind ourselves of something. Why do we need reminding? We know from our cycles of living for others or ourselves and then turning back the glory to God that we need a reminder for that turning. This reminder is that you matter. Your story—your life—you matter. Why does your story matter? I believe we are all created for the goodness and glory of God. God wanted the Israelites and Joshua to not only have a reminder of what God had done, but that God had done it for them.

Because they mattered.

We are all created in his image. If he made you like himself, you mean something. You are a human being in this world, you matter.

We are human. We are knowing and believing beings. We are storytellers. When we share our stories, we know and believe them to be true. When I tell my girls how God has provided for us again and again, I know it, I believe it, and therefore, I live it out. Alive and open to what he could do next. In turn, I hope they start to see it in their own lives and can share it with us and their friends.

Remember when I shared my tattoo as an Ebenezer? It reminded me that I was moving out of my deep depression. The other day I got my diploma in the mail for the master's program I just finished. It reminded me of another Ebenezer that I acquired during the time of this wilderness journey. It feels funny to say it, but it was *Frozen 2*.

As we know, 2018 had been a really difficult year for our family. The grief that led me into 2019 still grips me every once and a while. So, we ended 2018 and started 2019 with the best kind of trip. We went to Colorado and ended up getting snowed into our Airbnb. We could do nothing but read, play board games, stare out the window, and sit in the hot tub. It was a great way to start the new year. Throughout the year, I worked for a non-profit, taught online for Tulane University, and helped my sister and brother-in-law move cross-country to Seattle. I traveled for work and writing—even pitched this book idea to some publishers! On top of all of this, we decided to move. It was overall a busy but great, relaxing, and comfortable year.

While deciding to move, we also decided to go to Seattle for Thanksgiving to visit my sister and brother-in-law. We were all very excited about this trip. We planned for hiking, sitting and watching the snow fall outside the window, delicious food, and some touristy things. We also surprised the girls and bought tickets for us to see *Frozen 2* together.

All of it was amazing. The most beautiful hikes gave us visions of wandering through Narnia when the Pevensie children discovered it fresh out of the wardrobe. We ate great food, but honestly, the best meal was leftover turkey sandwiches from Thanksgiving after one of the hikes while it snowed. It was a refreshing time for a wonderfully busy year. A year in which I found myself to be very content.

Then we went to see *Frozen 2*. It was fun to have a night out with all of us. I had prepared one of our girls for what would happen to Olaf in the movie. She has a tender heart, and so do I; we both needed to know he would be okay. Friends, I cried like a baby. Like almost through the whole thing.

Why? Why?! I kept asking myself throughout the movie. Why was I so blubbery? It's just a kid's movie! But honestly, kids movies hit the hardest (don't even get me started on Moana). As I processed in real-time, I realized I had not fully processed all the grief from the previous year, and I was content with that. I did not want to change anything! In no way did I want to enter into the unknown. I just had this feeling, this weight, this something in the pit of my stomach that I was going to say yes to something unknown. I could not shake the feeling.

Here are a few thoughts on why, based on some of the songs.

"Some Things Never Change"

A little ditty letting you know everything is about to change. Change is inevitable, sometimes sooner than you think.

"Into the Unknown"

Not wanting change to impact what is good right now and making sure people don't think you are crazy for hearing things they can't hear. Listening to the song today brings excitement for the unknown, not fear. When I first heard the song, I had a deep fear that if I changed anything in our lives, it would ruin them even though I did not know what was going to change! I also had a fear of what people thought of me. I was still figuring out how to navigate that type of people-pleasing.

"The Next Right Thing"

Anna confesses her depression in the grief of losing her sister and Olaf. It's beautiful and heart-wrenching. It still makes me cry. I had begun getting serious about writing and was trying to figure out how to talk about depression and anxiety. This song showed me it was time to share it, and people needed to know they were not alone in those feelings. It is okay to express feelings that feel too big.

All these things helped me be mindful of what was happening around me. When the girls wanted to listen to the soundtrack, I would sing with them and ponder. I worked through these thoughts, journaling and asking God what was next.

What happened next? Little did we know we all needed the lessons of *Frozen 2* in 2020. But right before the pandemic kicked off, I got an email about a graduate school program.

When I got the email, I remembered that when this program first started, I was interested but had put it out of my mind. Our youngest was not in school yet, my husband was traveling, and I knew I wouldn't have the time or energy to do it well. It was simply not good timing. In January 2020, when I received the email, I remembered the longing to go back to school. The week before I received the email I was setting up my class to teach for the spring. That gut feeling hit again, and I wondered, *Am I teaching the wrong subject?*

I applied for the program that week. I decided to quit teaching the history of graphic design in May, so I could dive into learning. In the fall of 2020, I began the program for a Master's in Evangelism and Leadership. I finished in the fall of 2023. As I wrapped up that semester, I was wondering what was next. I was excited for more unknowns!

Sometimes, we may not see anything drastic or miraculous happening in our lives. I know God has moved in all aspects of my life. In ways I believe that no person or thing could. He has shown me that I matter to him. I perceive it. I have hope because of it, and sometimes, it's in seemingly small things like paying attention to a movie.

The wonder has called me to share. The Ebenezers in my life remind me to share my story of how God has cared for me and is caring for you. You may say that your story is not big enough or that it's too much to share. Who says so? I can tell you that God will never tell you those things. Let us choose to shift our perspective together and start living like our lives are worthy stories to tell because God says so.

If and when you fall into the lie of "your story is not big enough" or "it is too tough to handle," you will now be able to recognize that fall. Because you have looked back on your story, you realize the negative effects of living out that lie, and you will want to run away as fast as you can. If you don't, it can debilitate you from doing good—which is exactly what Satan wants. You know this; do not be okay with Satan trapping you.

I fall back into my old self in times of stress, but I must choose to step into the newness and not fall back into bondage. Jesus has overcome it, and I can lean on him as I walk through this stressful time. In my weakness, I am stronger with him.

One of the many ways we can live fully alive, doing good for the glory of God, is by sharing how God has moved in our lives. That is blessing him and bringing him glory. We do things out of our love for God because of his love for us which is glorious and glorifies him. It's that easy. But not that easy. It's not something that has to be world-changing.

But just maybe, sharing our story is life-changing.

We may have ten things shouting at us to be afraid, to turn and go back to our old ways, or fight battles we know we shouldn't. Maybe there are two things/people/spiritual gifts that can help us find the courage to continue our journey.

things to think about

I hope and pray God shows up for you
and you can notice how he is moving.

1. Do you have ways to pay attention to wonder and awe around you?

2. What are physical ways to help you remember?

Sidenote: Sometimes our stories are entangled in others lives and it can be hard to decide what is yours to share. If you feel it is time to share your story talk with God, perhaps that person, and a few wise, trusted friends. Maybe there is a way to share your story without the other, or you can come to an agreement of what is okay to share.

fourteen

how Jesus helps us live fully alive

*But, indeed, for this reason I have allowed you to remain, in order
to show you my power and in order to proclaim my name through
all the earth. (Exodus 9:16)*

We have looked at who you are and who God says you are.
We have begun to pay attention to how God is moving in and
around your story maybe choosing to mark specific instances
where we really see him move. We have looked at what drives
us and how we can be confident in him. Now, let's wrap up our
journey together!

The Israelites are in the promised land! They crossed the
Jordan River and are ready to do what is next. What I find in-
teresting is how two and a half of the tribes have already found
the land they would like to have. It's on the other side of the

Jordan where they just came from. Joshua asked them to come alongside the rest of the crew and help them receive the land that was promised to each of them—then they may return home.

I love this coming alongside. I believe we can do that, too. As we learn to walk in this new freedom of doing good for the glory of God alone, we will come alive! We have put aside the distractions of living to please others. Now we can do what God has asked us to do and aid those who are figuring out what God has called them to do. This essentially is mentorship, but fighting alongside and helping others find what good they are to do, is also camaraderie and what we so desperately need in our communities. The things we are passionate about and what calls to us can be so wildly different. I don't always understand the rigor and hardships of my friends' jobs, families, etc. But I do know that I love them and will always be there to lift them up, listen, or help them fight for God's glory in their story.

While crossing the Jordan into what felt like my (for now) promised land, I was in the middle of graduate school. I felt that tug from the Holy Spirit to let go of something again. It wasn't pride this time, it was something close to my heart that I loved. Remember those stories of Burundi? Well, after that first trip, I ended up working for that non-profit, Hope4Burundi, as the communications director. I got to tell their stories for a living. It was a joy.

The organization was about to make a major change in leadership. My parents were going to take over for the founders who were ready to retire. I was excited to work with them and keep on going! But in February 2022, I attended a conference, and I clearly heard God tell me to trust him and that it was time for me to go. I didn't want to leave my work. I procrastinated as long as I could just to double-check and make sure what I heard was true. It was. There is no denying it when you hear a still, small voice in the middle of worship. So, I listened. I was able to come alongside my parents for a bit as they stepped into something that has helped them live their most alive and glory-to-God life.

And because I listened? I did some grieving for the thing I loved. I began to live and do the good works for the glory of God. I had time to fully lean into school. I was able to complete a Bible study with my friend—we wrote it, I designed it, then we taught it for our church. I saw God weaving all the things into one as I began teaching what I knew I was called to, Jesus.

When you have decided to do things for the glory of God alone, you will have some doubts, and you will have some thoughts that you are crazy. I don't think I'm the only one. Feel free to ask some other people about it. I did! I have said no to things that make sense for this world: like jobs that make good money or saying no to things I love. During each of these big or small decisions, I could feel overwhelmed or walk in confidence.

What needs to happen is for me to seek God's wisdom, lean on my faith, and know that he can help me make the decision. And when I don't know what to say, the Holy Spirit guides and speaks on my behalf.

I don't usually make decisions because of some visible or audible thing God has given me. To be honest, it's usually a gut reaction. Over the past many years, I have learned that my gut reactions are usually indicators from the Holy Spirit. There is an idea in James 1:5-8 about choosing not to doubt when you ask for wisdom in faith. It tells us that if we lack wisdom, we should talk to God! He loves giving us what we are searching for. We are to do it out of faith, too—so without doubt (this is tough for a lot of us) and no second guessing. If we are double-minded, living with one foot in and and one foot out the door, we are unstable and will not receive the wisdom we ask for.

When I ask God to help me make a decision, what does it look like? Scripture doesn't say we need to plead to God in his goodness and mercy so that he grants all the good things. No, it says if you lack wisdom or clarity, ask for it without doubting. I'd like to add that at the end of those verses, it says to do it without assuming you will receive something in return for asking. In short, send up the ask, know what you are asking for, and be confident in it. I've learned over time that my unbelief makes me unsteady in my heart and actions. If I do not know what to believe, how can I stand strong? If I know what I believe but do not walk in it, I am not strong. I am also not looking for my strength. I am looking for his. I am asking him to help me with my unbelief.

Jesus had promised the Holy Spirit to his disciples and then to anyone who would believe in his name from there on out. Jesus was leaving the Holy Spirit, one of the Triune God, on this planet within humans to help guide us. Why is it so important that Jesus leaves and the Spirit comes? We don't get to reach the promised land until his second return. We need some guidance. And everything in the Bible shows this relationship with God moving closer and closer to now when the Spirit is in us and coming alongside us.

In Acts 2, the Holy Spirit descended with a mighty gushing wind, tongues of fire, and then rested on all the men and women believers in the home. It was the day of Pentecost 10 days after Jesus had left them. All the believers spoke different languages telling of wonders and God's goodness to the crowds filling Jerusalem for this annual festival. People heard about Jesus in their own tongue! Some marveled. Some thought the believers were drunk.

When we follow Jesus, we might look a little weird. A little wild. A little on fire. One thing for sure is doing good for his glory and not worrying about the opinions of others. Jesus leaving us helps us live fully alive through his death, resurrection, ascension, and the sending of the Holy Spirit to indwell us.

Just like Moses put Joshua in charge of helping the Israelites flourish in the land given to them, Jesus put the disciples in charge of furthering the gospel and glory of God into the whole world.

As the Israelites wrapped up their story for now, they moved through the promised land claiming the land. They still had moments of complaints and complacency and saw plenty of miracles. One of them was when the sun stood still for a day! They began to get comfortable in their new land and didn't quite get to all the land they were to receive. They settled down, and the two and a half tribes returned home east of the Jordan. Joshua recounted the story of the Israelites in a "Cliff Notes" version, from Abraham to Egypt, the wilderness, and where they were now. He called them to choose who they would serve and told them that he and his house would choose God. He hoped they would, too. He reminded them they must stop idolatry, remember their identity as holy set apart people to rest and prosper in the land God had given them.

Jesus sent the disciples out and gave them the decree to proclaim the gospel to all creation. No specific way. He gave them all they needed to move forward with their good work. Some for teaching, missions work, cooking, hosting, creating, and the list goes on. They came alongside each other learning, praying, eating, and helping each other pay their bills. Community.

God trusts us. Whew. That's wild.

I will not find the ultimate promised land. I am okay with that. Are you? What do I mean by that? Well, our promised land isn't here on this earth; it comes after the new Jerusalem arrives. (Head on over to Revelation for that. I will not be going there.) My point is that we will not reach perfection, the best job, or our most passionate perfect calling. We can get close, and when working with God and for his glory, we will see glimpses of those things. And when you do, take note and remember.

He is good to us and wants all the good things for us, but since this world is broken, we don't get to be perfect while we are here walking around. I think that it's good for us because no one will be able to boast or brag about being the ultimate perfect human. Jesus is the only one who gets to claim that.

He wants us to be the ones to bring the good news to those who are struggling in this world. The good news of Jesus, the only perfect human, someone we can never be. If we look to him, we can see how he didn't aim to please those around him. He sought God in the quiet space or up on the mountain. He rested, he pursued his friends, he loved those who were not loved. He brought beauty to being a human. God's work is perfect, and my work is good because of him. We get to come alongside him to do good and mighty works.

We will always be in the midst of ongoing supernatural work that is God setting us apart as holy in this world. The story doesn't end here. I also believe that we will go through wilderness journeys as we move, grow, and lean more into God. Perfection only comes when we get to heaven and get our new digs. So go live life, my friends. God is pleased with you; you do not need to look to another. Keep your eyes on him.

Your journey has not ended; it has only begun. I hope you can reflect on what God has done in your life and how he is forming you to do the good works set before you. Get excited about stepping forward in this wholeness! May you go in peace.

things to think about

I hope and pray God shows up for you
and you can notice how he is moving.

1. Do you believe you are who God says you are?

2. How do you feel to know that God trusts you?

Acknowledgments

Let us first acknowledge—an acknowledgment section of a book is a nightmare for recovering people-pleasers. I shall keep it short and sweet. I know I'll forget to thank someone(s), so I hope and pray that if you are reading this page, you know you have impacted me. I hope I have the chance to hug you and say thank you to your most gracious face. Thank you to all who endured some raw, extreme, I-am-gonna-quit moments and encouraged me to keep going.

Eric, Ella, and Mia – There are not enough pages to say thank you for how much time and resources you gave up for me to write this book. Girls, more than you will ever know this book is for you. So that you may live free and your most alive life. Eric, thank you for the conversation that one night in the kitchen where you told me to start writing or stop talking about it. I hope you know I will always be writing and talking about it. Thank you for the gift of believing in the work put before me when so many thought we were crazy. I love you and I like you.

The Family – Thank you for your sacrifices and for being available and willing to care for E and M. Thank you for reading my work and being excited about it, even when it wasn't great. Thank you for filling our bellies when I was busy. Thank you for taking us on vacations and good trips, many of which gave my brain space for my writing to flourish.

Besties – Saying we have been through a lot in the last few years is an understatement. Whether we communicate by sharing weighty text messages or funny but true reels on Instagram, and whenever we accomplish the impossible by getting our open days to match up, I'm grateful for living life with y'all. There is not enough charcuterie, chips and queso, coffee, or mixed drinks to thank you for all you have done.

Propel 4 Cohort – The collective wisdom, conversations, challenges, and laughter have made me and this book better. Our three years together are one of the things I will forever cherish.

Editor, Steph – Thank you for being willing and available to work with this newbie. I appreciate your kindness, honesty, and helping my author's voice come through.

Punchline Publishers – Joy and Amelia. Without your guidance and punctuality, I don't know that this book would have made it into the world. I have so much respect for what you do. Thank you for taking a chance on me!

This book could not have happened without the love and support of all those in my life. Thank you!

notes

Chapter 2

1. Douglas S. Huffman and Jamie N. Hausherr, "Manna," ed. John D. Barry et al., *The Lexham Bible Dictionary* (Bellingham, WA: Lexham Press, 2016).

2. Hagberg, Janet O., and Robert A. Guelich. *The Critical Journey: Stages in the Life of Faith. 2nd ed.* (Salem: Sheffield Publishing Company, 2004), 45.

Chapter 7

1. Crouch, Andy. *Culture Making: Recovering Our Creative Calling.* (IVP Books, 2013.), page 252.

Chapter 10

1. Smith, Gordon T. *Beginning Well: Christian Conversion & Authentic Transformation.* (Downers Grove, Ill: IVP Books, 2001), page 132.

Chapter 11

1. Crouch, Andy. *Culture Making: Recovering Our Creative Calling.* (IVP Books, 2013.), page 261.

about the author

Heather Seeger is an author, graphic designer, and former adjunct professor with Master's degrees in both Graphic Communications and Evangelism and Leadership. She is the author of *People Please! Leaving the Crowd's Approval for the Glory of One, Bible 101: Understand the Bible's Framework from Genesis to Revelation*, and has contributed to several other works.

After living as a chronic people pleaser for decades, Heather discovered the freedom that came with finding her identity only in pleasing Christ. Through her writing, Heather hopes to help other Christian women turn away from living for others and place their confidence in the identity that only comes from God.

Aside from writing, Heather finds peace and healing when she's in nature (thanks to her Colorado roots), spending time with friends and family, and watching shows and movies that she can squeeze theological meaning from. Heather now lives outside of Austin, Texas with her husband, Eric, two middle school daughters, and a dog. When she isn't writing or designing, you can find her teaching middle school Sunday school or Bible studies for women in her local church.

Connect with Heather

heatherseeger.com

▤ heatherseeger.substack.com

◎ heather_seeger

Great books are even better when they're shared!

Help other readers find this book!

- Post a review on your favorite online bookseller
- Post a picture on a social media account, share why you liked it, and tag the author!
- Send a note to a friend who would also love it—or better yet, give them a copy.

Thank you for reading!

Heather Seeger

www.ingramcontent.com/pod-product-compliance
Lightning Source LLC
Chambersburg PA
CBHW051005140626
46546CB00016B/506